Patterns of Destruction:
Counseling for Victims of Family Violence

By

Stan E. DeKoven

Patterns of Destruction:
Counseling for Victims of
Family Violence

Copyright © 1994
Vision Publishing
Ramona, CA 92065

Revised addition 2010

All rights in this book are reserved world-wide.
No part of the book may be reproduced in any manner whatsoever without written permission of the author except in brief quotations embodied in critical articles of reviews.

ISBN: 978-1-61529-011-6

For information on reordering please contact:

Vision Publishing
1115 D Street
Ramona, CA 92065
1-800-9-VISION
www.visionpublishingservices.com

All scripture references are taken from the New American Standard Bible unless otherwise noted.

Acknowledgments

The author would like to acknowledge the Staff of Vision International University, especially Dr. Joseph Bohac for his assistance with this manuscript. Further, my deepest thanks and eternal affection to my own family, Karen, Rebecca and Rachel, for their loving support. Finally, to the hundreds of victims and perpetrator victims who have taken courageous steps towards recovery during years of counseling practice. May the Lord use this manuscript for healing and understanding.

Table of Contents

Introduction: The Family Violent 7
Ch. 1 God's Agenda for the Family 11
Ch. 2 The Nature of Family Violence 17
Ch. 3 Family Stress and Distress 33
Ch. 4 Family Communication and Violence 43
Ch. 5 Spousal Abuse: Dynamics of Rage 49
Ch. 6 Alcohol/Drugs and Abuse 59
Ch. 7 Adolescent Violence in the Family 65
Ch. 8 Child Abuse 71
Ch. 9 Sexual Abuse 81
Ch. 10 The Results of Abuse 91
Ch. 11 Crisis Management 99
Ch. 12 Treatment Process 111
Ch. 13 Major Modes of Marital Counseling 119
Ch. 14 Assisting to Rebuild Violent Family Systems 137
Ch. 15 The Secret Revealed: Facing the Truth 147
Ch. 16 Decontamination: The Cleansing 159
Ch. 17 Direction: New Beginnings 167
Ch. 18 The Church's Response: A Wake Up Call 171
Case Studies
    1. 179
    2. 183
Bibliography 187
Additional References 191
Appendices 195

Introduction:
The Family Violent

It was 1984 when my former associate and I first began working as counselors with the Domestic Violence and Youth Diversion programs of the San Diego City Police Department. I never thought that much of my focus in therapy over the next few years would be with victims of family abuse, either past or present.

My leading in that direction should not have seemed such a surprise. We had long been desirous of developing our counseling ministry with specializations in what seemed to be the most needed fields of concern: dysfunctional families, adult children of alcoholics, adults molested as children, etc. These kinds of individual and family problems had for some time been on a steady increase. Yet, my personal interest stemmed from my own family background, since my family of origin was intensely dysfunctional and frequently disruptive. This is not necessarily the best reason to develop a counseling practice or ministry, but the combination of the exercise of personal demons and clinical training has been highly therapeutic for many, including me. My hope is that my knowledge and experience will be expressed in wisdom for those who suffer and for clinicians and pastors who desire to be "wounded healers."

How to Use this Book and the Study Guide

First, this manuscript is written for those preparing themselves for effective counseling ministry in this growing arena of concern. This manuscript was meant to be used with the study guide and teaching/seminar tapes provided for students matriculating in University or Bible College programs. The focus is to first present the various facts and figures related to family violence, and then to provide various plans of intervention for families caught in the web of violence.

Secondly, in the section on victims and victimizers, the dynamics of abuse in various areas is fully detailed.

Finally, the section on treatment and recovery details the process of change. The strategies presented are tested over time, and useful for most people, perpetrators and victims alike. When combined with God's power and good clinical wisdom, positive and permanent results glorifying to the Lord will be the result. It is my hope that the reader will grow as he/she processes through the material.

"Then God said, 'Let us make man in our image, according to Our likeness; and let them rule over the fish of the sea and over the birds of the sky and over the cattle and over all the earth, and over every creeping thing that creeps on the earth.' God created man in His own image, in the image of God He created him; male and female He created them."

"The Lord God fashioned into a woman the rib which He had taken from the man, and brought her to the man. The man said
'This is now bone of my bones, And flesh of my flesh; She shall be called Woman Because she was taken out of Man.'"

"For this cause a man shall leave his father and his mother, and be joined to his wife; and they shall become one flesh. And the man and his wife were both naked and were not ashamed."

Genesis 1:26-27, 2:22-25

*It is a reverent thing to see an ancient castle
or building not in decay: or to see a fair
timber tree sound and perfect.
How much more to behold an ancient and noble
Family which hath stood against the waves and
Weathers of time.*
Sir Francis Bacon: *Essays*

Chapter 1
God's Agenda for the Family

In the author's book, *Turning Points,*[1] the family is described as God's primary unit for socialization. It was created, not as an afterthought, but as a part of God's original plan. From the beginning, God created the family as a primary institution for the training and development of all human beings. We find this illustrated very clearly in the Genesis account of God's creation of the family unit (Chapters 2 and 3).

A family is not just a collection of individuals, but a system of people who interact with one another. A family is a unit, with mutual dependency and patterns of interaction unique to its' own. Each individual member, as they interact, impact the others in a profound manner. There is no greater or more significant relationship that is developed in human terms than that of the family.

It is also true that the body of Christ has been described rightly so as a family for the people of God. Whether the spiritual family created by God or the natural family system we were raised with, none is perfect. We must, as Christian Caregivers, recognize that the best of all parents are far from perfect. Therefore, the needs that we have for significance, acceptance, and approval cannot be fully met within our family of origin. This is one of the reasons the

---

[1] *Turning Points,* Stan DeKoven, Ph.D. Vision Publishing, p 64

whole human family is in desperate need of God's gracious salvation provided through Christ. We need Christ, and we also need family, designed by God both naturally and spiritually. Unfortunately, the family units we become a part of, designed by God for our nurture and delight can also become the hot bed for hurt and wounds.

When families are not functioning well, the balance of the system, the homeostatic balance can be upset. At times an identified patient can emerge. For example, with families with teenage children, one of the teenagers may begin to act out. They may run away, do drugs or alcohol, etc. Much of this acting out behavior is no doubt caused by peer temptations, a primary attempt of the enemy of our souls to divide and disrupt family life. However, many times their aggressive behavior can be a symptom of a family not functioning at its' optimum. When the later is the case, we as ministers of counseling must realize that the whole family is in crisis, not just an individual member. Pastors and counselors are thus tasked with the responsibility of assisting the whole family system without judgment or condemnation.

Family and Violence. These two words should never be found in the same sentence, yet each day all around the world wives are physically, emotionally and sexually battered and abused by their husbands. Husbands and wives are attacked by out of control adolescents; children are neglected, abused and sexually traumatized, leaving life-long scars on the victims. This was certainly not God's plan for mankind and the family unit.

God's intention, as seen in Genesis 1 and 2, Ephesians 5, Colossians 3 and I Peter 3 as well as many other passages in the Word (see the appendix for a fairly comprehensive review of scriptures on marriage and family), was for husbands and wives to love and nurture one another, and for children to be raised in a truly nurturing, loving environment.[2] The fall of man, caused by

---

[2] For more on God's agenda for the family, see the author's book "Marriage and Family Life: A Christian Perspective."

disobedience, has so tainted the world that the ideal of scripture (or even television with families like the Waltons, Father Knows Best, Leave It To Beaver and The Brady Bunch) seems virtually impossible. Yet, God's plan is for families to fulfill their call, as living examples in a sin-stained and torn world. Regardless of past circumstances, cultural values, individual differences, or psychological deficits, God desires to bring the family to wholeness through the power of Jesus Christ.

Defining Terms

For many the following <u>definitions</u> can be helpful as we begin our study together. They are taken largely from Funk and Wagnall's Standard Dictionary:

1. **Family.** 1. Parents and their children, 2. The children as distinguished from the parents, 3. A group of persons connected by blood or marriage, 4. A succession of persons connected by blood, name, etc. a house, a clan, 5. Distinguished or ancient lineage or descent, 6. A household, 7. Any class or group of like or related things.

    I would add to this list of <u>definitions</u> by including, "a constitution of members by blood or law, to include parents and children whether natural, adoptive or foster children".

2. **Violence.** 1. The quality or state of being violent, intensity, fury. 2. An instance of violent action, treatment, etc. 3. Violent or abusive exercises of power, injury, outrage. 4. Law, physical force unlawfully exercised. 5. Perversion or distortion of meaning, intent, etc. To injure or damage by rough or abusive treatment.

    To those violated, the intense violent and abusive exercise of power to create injury has caused extreme damage (trauma). This creates a sense of justifiable outrage in the victim and shame (we would hope) in the victimizer.

3. **Abuse.** 1. To use improperly or injuriously; misuse. 2. To hurt by treating wrongly, injure. 3. To speak in coarse or bad terms of or to revile; ill treatment. 4. Vicious conduct, practice or action. 5. Abusive language; slander. Abuse can be both verbal and physical, perpetrated by the stronger upon the weaker.
4. **Neglect.** 1. To fail to heed or take note of or disregard. 2. To fail to give proper attention to; to neglect ones business. 3. To fail to perform; leave undone. Noun: 1. Habitual want of attention or care; negligence. 2. The act of neglecting, or the state of being neglected. 3. An instance of neglect.

Many victims of neglect (usually children) have stated emphatically that they preferred abuse to neglect. That is, negative attention is more tolerable than no attention at all.

Family violence occurs whenever one member of the family is violated or neglected by another (or in sexual abuse outside of the family, the whole family is victimized) who is in a position to act differently, and where normal societal expectations are such that they allow for the different behavior. Family violence is on the increase in all segments of society, and affects everyone.

Galatians 6:1 states that we are to restore (return to God's original intent) those who are caught in any sin. Further II Corinthians 1:3 states that we are to comfort those who need comfort. Thus, the plan and purpose of God would be two fold.

1. Restoration for the Perpetrator (who in most cases was a victim themselves)
2. Comfort and Reconciliation for the victim (without which the cycle of abuse is likely to continue).

We will discuss more on this in the segment on treatment.

For Class Discussion

1. Discuss the similarities and dissimilarities between the Body of Christ as a family and the human family.

2. Discuss each of the terms defined and relate to situations in your own experience.

3. Discuss any experiences you may have had with programs aimed at restoration.

"If you strike a child, take care that you strike in anger, even at the risk of maiming it for life. A Blow in cold blood neither can nor should be forgiven."
George Bernard Shaw, "How to Beat a Child"

"Foolishness is bound up in the heart of a child; The rod of discipline will remove it far from him."

Proverbs 22:15

"Do not associate with a man *given* to anger; Or go with a hot-tempered man, Or you will learn his ways, And find a snare for yourself."

Proverbs 22:24-25

For son treats father contemptuously,
Daughter rises up against her mother,
Daughter-in-law against her mother-in-law;
A man's enemies are the men of his own household.
Micah 7:6

Chapter 2
The Nature of Family Violence

In 1976, 1 out of 26 wives (3.8%) annually or 1.8 million women were physically or sexually assaulted by their spouses. Over 30% of females who were murdered in America were killed by their husbands. It is estimated that presently between 12-15 million abuse cases occur in the United States annually, but less than 2% are ever reported (Geller, 1992).

In a more updated report, Bohovec states that "physical violence occurs in 50% of all marriages and severe physical violence occurs in 25% of marriages" (Bohovec, 1994). The level of violence and its causes are multiple, as we shall see later.

The incidence of abuse, especially sexual abuse of children, is alarming. It is reported commonly that approximately 40% of all females and 20-25% of all males have been sexually violated before the age of 18. Of those who are abused, 81% were abused before puberty and 42% before the age of 7 (Finkelhor, 1984).

Abuse is not just a problem in America, or amongst only one cultural group. Sexual abuse and violence crosses cultural and socio-economic classes.

For example, child marriage is the rule in India. The tradition of *purdah* (seclusion of girls) requires marriage as early as age 6 or 7 (Journal of Psychohistory, 1991). This highly common occurrence introduces young girls to adult sexual activity at an age that mars their ability to experience mature and healthy sexual expression. This early and inappropriate tradition sets the stage for the inability of the female parent to effectively protect their daughters of the next generation.

Within the Latin culture (including Latin America and nations under Latin influence, such as Philippines, Guam, etc.) the rate of incest is alarmingly high. There is a perceived danger of seduction by fathers and step-fathers (often unmarried partners, since divorce is not permitted by the Catholic Church), older brothers, etc.

In Europe, the problem exists as well. Though the figures are difficult to obtain in communist nations, approximately 300,000 reported and confirmed cases of the sexual abuse of children occur each year. This in societies that tend to under report such events (Journal of Psychohistory, 1991).

Finally, in other industrialized and third world nations, incest, sexual exploitation of children, the mistreatment and disrespect of women is well known. Unfortunately, the brokenness of our world often becomes most clearly evident in the homes of people, even among Christian families.

The Nature of Violence

The facts speak for themselves. The incidence of Family Violence and related issues are endemic in Western culture, and in the Two-Thirds world. (Brewer, C., 1990)

Causes of Abusive Families

There are several characteristics of abusive family systems. Firstly, victims of childhood abuse frequently find victimizers to marry. It is hypothesized that this occurs out of an unconscious desire to "heal themselves" or perpetuate their ingrained (known and thus comfortable) belief system. That is, the victim believes that if he or she can make his or her spouse love them, then all of the wounds of the past will be eradicated. This is referred to as "magical thinking." Unfortunately, because of past abuse or neglect, low self-esteem develops, creating an underlying belief that "no one could ever love me." This traumatic bonding is most detrimental.

Secondly, society, and even the church, perpetuates certain roles, beliefs and values that are anti-Biblical and stereotypically dysfunctional. This includes the concept of the parents "right of entitlement" or ownership of their children, allowing them to treat them as they like without the slightest concern for the consequences. The biblical mandate to spare the rod or spoil the child has been interpreted as a right to hit at will, rather than a mandate to teach and train children to be respectful adults. Further, communication (discussed more fully in the section on family communication) is clearly different in abusive and neglectful families. Frequently, neither couple had adequate role modeling to know what good communication was (or what a good marriage was, for that matter).

Finally, inappropriate expectations and poor impulse control, combined with significant family stress can lead to the family violence cycle. Rage, the out of control expression of intense anger, can be overwhelming, and is the outgrowth of significant character deficits in the abuser, often "brought out" by the victim. These patterns are often seen generationally (Exodus 20:34) in that "the sin of the fathers are perpetuated," as in "like produces like."

Rage and its' expression is one of the key ingredients of family violence. Goldberg discusses rage in the following terms:

"The accumulation of rage in intimate, bonded, heterosexual relationships is built-in, and in direct proportion to the extent of the man's 'masculine' defenses and the woman's 'feminine' defenses. It is a paradoxical and painful irony that the more classically romantic the relationship is at its onset, the more the phenomenon of rage building up holds true....

"To understand this buildup of rage, we need to look at the defensive processes involved in the gender conditioning we term masculinity and femininity. Traditionally, femininity involves a number of basic areas of repression. Little girls are taught to repress their sexuality (it's okay to be cuddly, but not "horny") to repress anger ("to be sugar and spice and everything nice") and to repress their assertiveness..." (Goldberg, pp. 61-64).

Likewise, masculinity is a set of defenses against dependency, emotionalism in general, vulnerability, passivity, absence of sexuality, fear, etc. A "real man" validates himself as "masculine" if he doesn't really need anybody, never lets conditions interfere with his responses, is "afraid of nothing," rarely tires, is always decisive, knows what to do and how to take charge, and is always ready sexually and able to perform with prowess and expertise."

Goldberg goes on to say that "romance is a process of a man and a woman falling in love with each other's defenses" (Goldberg, 1992). It is only later that she begins to resent some of the very qualities that attracted her in the first place. The man is initially drawn to the woman's emotionality, which he later comes to consider as childishness.

According to Goldberg, "rage builds up as they come to see each other as blocks to personal growth".

Case in Point:
George and Mary Ann

This couple, ages 26 and 24, were referred for counseling by their pastor. They had been married for four years and were committed Christians. The pastor related that the clients were in need of counseling because the husband was beginning to "lose it," yelling and threatening his wife. The precipitating event included a protracted screaming match, culminating in George punching a hole in the wall of their kitchen (he stated it was better than punching her face! No doubt!).

George was initially the primary spokesman for the family, explaining and projecting blame for his behavior. He did not want to be angry, was ashamed but lacked the awareness of his part in the conflict. Mary Ann had accepted most of the responsibility for the problems, with promises to change. Neither could declaratively state how they got to this place, since they loved each other romantically and intently.

Our initial counseling explored the beginning of their relationship. They both related that they knew that God had ordained their marriage and were very much in love (romantically) with each other. Their intimate (sexual) relationship was intense and satisfying (even after the last acting out segment). We further discussed their family of origin, family models, style of communication and problem solving skills. What we learned was most revealing.

George was the oldest child and the only son. He related that his father was a hard worker but emotionally distant, whereas he was the "apple of his mother's eye." She was devoted to him, establishing a certain amount of narcissistic dependency and expectancy of special treatment.

Mary Ann was also the oldest child, but was the primary caretaker for the younger siblings. Her mother had been severely ill, and she "accepted" her role as mother surrogate for the family. Her relationship with her father was very close and dependent, in that he was dependent on her for emotional support and "comfort." There was no indication of abuse, but some "emotional incest" was evident.

When George and Mary Ann got married, the romantic excitement of their union carried them for almost their first year. If there ever was conflict they would merely overlook it. Initially, George's dependence and demanding of Mary Ann's attention and affection (he could not seem to do anything for himself) and Mary Ann's competence and smothering were quite acceptable. However, over time the mothering felt like smothering and the demanding felt like neglect/abuse. This, over time, led to the present situation. This is typical of many couples on the road toward domestic violence. Fortunately, their early intervention proved most helpful. Through counseling they learned to develop boundaries and....

In Goldberg's research he observed that the repressed rage responses of a woman in the following behaviors:

1. Passive Aggression -- This is a showing of anger (rage) by always being late, procrastination, non-responsiveness, etc.
2. Lack of Energy -- the woman being exhausted most of the time, thus unable to perform her duties as wife and/or mother.
3. Psychosomatic Complaints – whereby the woman exhibits an ever increasing list of symptoms and imaginary illnesses.
4. Religious Fanaticism, mysticism, and moral righteousness -- Which was used as a way to gain power in the relationship.
5. Complaining and nagging--usually about the same or similar things which are generally unchangeable in the man or originally valued behaviors.
6. Crying, blaming and other emotional displays of pain and hurt--designed to make him feel guilty and shamed.
7. Emotional Breakdown--which is not caused by legitimate psychological or physiological stressors.
8. Helplessness and Fear -- as a sign of dependency and to manipulate the spouse to provide desired attention.
9. Compulsive Homemaking and Mothering -- which is most irritating and annoying to the husband and out of balance to the family needs.

On the other hand Goldberg sees the masculine expressions of rage as:

1. Withdrawal and non-responsiveness – demonstrated by the fact that the angrier he feels, the colder and more detached he becomes. He may tend to become a "couch potato."
2. Paternalism – characterized by demeaning putdowns of her behaviors, look or style.

3. Critical and Sarcastic Humor – often expressed in public and in front of children.
4. Intellectualization -- never discusses feelings, but rather intellectualizes everything.
5. Passive Indifference -- and I don't care about you or your problems attitude.
6. Insensitivity -- repeatedly tries to hurt her through cutting words or disregarding her needs and feelings.
7. Workaholism–a passive-aggressive and avoidant behavior.
8. Self-destructiveness and Impulsiveness -- drinks too much, gambles, etc.

Goldberg formulated that "Spousal violence is the product of an interaction or rhythm between two people who are intensely dependent on each other and yet feel trapped, frustrated, and disappointed with each other at the same time. This was certainly the case of George and Mary Ann. He wanted "freedom," but was intensely dependent on Mary Ann for "permission". She needed to be needed but resented his neediness.

The inevitable feelings of resentment and discouragement over attempting without success to make things better, combined with the deeper sense of being blocked by the other person from growing and becoming real, make the relationship volatile.

Goldberg suggested that the "ingredients" that set the stage for the rage that produces physical attack include:

> • A traditional woman whose childlike dependence and feelings of helplessness propel her to crave reassurance, contact, and closeness in a relationship with a machinelike male whose tendency is towards isolation. A vicious circle is created as she demands more and he wants less. While she complains of rejection, he complains of being smothered.
> • A traditional man and woman who are unable to fight fairly and resolve conflicts.

- An actor-reactor interaction that is basically boring to both, though neither has the resources to effectively change things.
- A traditional man and woman who are drawn to each other out of defensive needs and insecurity and are regressively dependent on each other.
- A man and woman who resent critical aspects of each other.
- A situation in which the same basic fights repeat themselves time and time again.
- A man who has needs but is fearful and unable to ask for what he wants, and resents it when he is not being correctly divined...a woman who has need for power and autonomy, but feels unable to directly take it and blames her husband for "controlling" her.
- A woman who knows what she doesn't like, but has difficulty defining what she wants.
- A relationship that begins on a tremendously high level of romantic attachment.
- Love, marriage and intimacy are different tasks to successfully negotiate in the healthiest of situations. When one or both people in a relationship have significant deficits in personality structure or socialization, the potential for explosive interaction eventuates.

Domestic Violence: Men Who Batter

A considerable amount of research has been presented in recent years attempting to shed some light on the causes of violent behavior in men, especially the behavior that results in domestic violence. In a workshop at the Conference on Trauma and Sexuality in San Diego in 1993, Douglas Humphries offered the following findings on men who batter (Humphries, 1993):

- Men who batter their wives often do not come across to those outside the family as abusive individuals. Frequently the abusive man maintains a public image as a friendly, caring person who is a devoted "family man" (David Adams, "Identifying the Assaultive Husband in Court: You Be the Judge," to be published in Boston Bar Journal. 1989, p.2).
- Batterers are reported to be seductive and charming when they are not being violent, and women fall for their short-lived but sincere promises. It seems unusual to have one-third of the sample pregnant at the time of their marriage to the batterer although we had no comparison data (Lenore Walker, "The Battered Woman Syndrome Study: Results and Discussion," Paper presented at the National Family Violence Research conference, Durham, NH, 1981, p. 10).
- Only 20 percent of the batterers are also violent to individuals outside the home. Many batterers have successful careers and are highly respected in their communities (Lenore Walker, Terrifying Love: Why Battered Women Kill and How Society Responds. NY: Harper & Row, Publishers, 1989. p. 71).
- In one study, only 20% of the batterers reportedly limited their violence towards their wives. The other 80% also engaged in violent behavior towards other targets, such as child and parent abuse, incest, harming pets, destroying objects, and acting abusively towards other people (Lenore Walker, "Eliminating Sexism to End Battering Relationships." Paper presented at the American Psychological Association, Toronto, ON. 1984. p. 2).
- For 39% of these men, their frustration led to

violence only in the presence of their wives or lovers; for 33%, their frustration led to violence only when they were in the presence of their partners, children, and mothers. In only 28% of these cases were the men violent both within and outside the family (James Ptacek, "Why Do Men Batter Their Wives? Chapter 6 from Feminist Perspectives on Wife Abuse, ed. Kersti Yllo and Michele Bogard, Newbury Park, CA: Sage Publications. 1988. p. 143).

• Dr. Daniel Sonkin, a San Francisco psychologist, found that 95 percent of men who sought treatment for their battering behavior admitted to abusing more than one woman. Likewise, Dr. Anne Ganley has found that the batterers she treated often go on to batter another woman in their next relationship. Each partner of the batterer is different enough in behavior and character for Dr. Ganley to have drawn the conclusion that the abusive behavior stems from the male batterer himself, not from the relationship (Walker, Terrifying Love. p. 72).

• Clinicians note that at least half of the small percentages of abusive men who receive treatment continue their violent behavior with new partners (Lenore Walker and Angela Browne, "Gender and Victimization by Intimates," draft version, published in Journal of Personality. Vol. 53. No. 2. 1985, p. 17).

• The particularly vicious batterer usually has a violent history (Berk, Berk, Loseke & Rama, 1983, from Jacquelyn C. Campbell, "If I Can't Have You, No One Can: Power and Control in Homicide of Female Partners," unpublished draft to be published in Femicide: The Politics of Woman Killing, ed. J.

Radford and D.E.H. Russell, Boston, MA: Twayne Publishers, p. 6).
- 72% of the batterers (in Walker's study) were arrested as compared to 34% of the non-batterers. 44% of those batterers arrested, as compared with 19% of the non-batterers, were convicted of those charges. These results support the belief that batterers as a group are a violent population (Walker, Terrifying Love. p. 22).
- Experts working with abusive men note that they greatly underreport their violent actions, minimizing or denying assaultive behavior against their wives, and claiming more involvement by the victim of their violence that witness or police reports would support (Irene Hanson Frieze and Angela Browne, "Violence in Marriage." Family Violence. ed. Lloyd Ohlin and Michael H. Tony. Chicago: University of Chicago Press. 1987. p. 7).
- Few, if any, abusive husbands characterize themselves as men who beat their wives. A recent informal poll of clients at Emerge revealed that few men, even the most severe abusers, had thought of themselves in those terms. The abuser's tendency to minimize problems is comparable to the denial problems of alcohol or drug abusers (Adams, "Identifying the Assaultive Husband in Court: You Be The Judge." p. 3).
- Descriptive studies emphasizing the psycho-pathological roots of battering traces male violence to a vulnerable self-concept (or low self-esteem); a complex of helplessness, powerlessness, or inadequacy; conflicts over being dependent; traditional attitudes, particularly about sex; pathological jealousy and fear of abandonment. These are alternated with desire for control over

women and children; an inability to communicate feelings or to identify feelings in others (empathy); and a lack of assertiveness (Evan Stark and Anne Flitcraft, "Violence Among Intimates: An Epidemiological Review," Chapter 13 from Handbook of Family Violence. Ed. Von Haselt, et. al. 1988. Incomplete Citation, p. 307).

• No factor other than male violence appears to precipitate any substantial degree of woman battering. Conversely, apart from age, no factors have been consistently found to increase a woman's risk of abuse. Race, income, occupation, alcohol, an inheritance of violence, isolation and status inconsistency are frequently cited risk factors, but their importance remains ambiguous (Stark and Flitcraft, "Violence Among Intimates." p. 307).

• Batterers tended to be less educated than their wives, from a lower socio-economic class, and from a different ethnic, religious, or racial group (Walker, "The Battered Woman Syndrome Study: Results and discussion." p. 9).

There is Nothing New Under the Sun

For even the casual observer of the word of God, violence is not new to the human condition. Shortly after the fall of man, as recorded in Genesis 3, family violence became an only too true reality. In Genesis 4, verses 1-9 we read the following:

"Now the man had relations with his wife Eve, and she conceived and gave birth to Cain, and she said "I have gotten a manchild with *the help of* the Lord." 2 Again, she gave birth to his brother Abel. And Abel was a keeper of flocks, but Cain was a tiller of the ground. 3 So it came about in the course of time that Cain brought an offering to the Lord of the fruit of the ground. 4 Abel, on his part also brought of the firstlings of his flock and of their fat portions. And the Lord had regard for Abel and for his offering; 5 but for Cain and for his offering He had no regard. So Cain became very angry and his countenance fell. 6 Then the Lord said to Cain, 'Why are you angry? And why has your countenance fallen? 7 If you do well, will not your countenance be lifted up? And if you do not do well, sin is crouching at the door; and its desire is for you, but you must master it" 8 Cain told Abel his brother. And it came about when they were in the field, that Cain rose up against Abel his brother and killed him. 9 Then the Lord said to Cain, 'Where is Abel your brother?' And he said, 'I do not know. Am I my brother's keeper?"

What excitement must have come to the house of Adam and Eve. Two sons, both with the ability to carry on the family name; destined to be co-laborers over all the family inheritance. Though we can only hypothesize the dialog in the family, it would be reasonable to assume that both boys knew about the problems of disobedience to the Lord as demonstrated in their parents' lives. It is also reasonable to assume that the offerings (to be the first fruits of their labor, presented by Abel but not Cain) were to be acts of worship and obedience practiced by the parents. However, Cain refused to follow the word of God fully, resulting in guilt and depression (a fallen countenance). As would have been true of brothers, Cain shared with his brother the hurt and anger towards God not regarding his offering, perhaps looking for sympathy from Abel. Apparently, sympathy was not received, perhaps increasing his anger. The scripture indicates that the Lord came to Cain, providing ample opportunity to repent of his rage. Though denied by men and women acting out in violence, the scripture clearly indicates that it was Cain's choice to act out or repent of his rage. How much more should we as Christians have control on our feelings and behavior by the power of the Holy Spirit. His act was made worse by his attitude expressed in his rhetorical question, "Am I my brother's keeper?" He and all who act out in the family are without excuse.

As we will see in the rest of the study, there is actually no excuse for acting out against ones family in violence. No excuse can be given a client who has followed in the footsteps of Cain. Facing the truth, accepting the consequences, and working out ones salvation with fear and trembling is absolutely necessary for healing in the broken, violent home.

For Class Discussion

1. Discuss the causes and characteristics of abusive family systems.

2. Discuss the "repressed responses by women" as suggested by Goldberg.

3. Discuss the masculine expressions of rage as suggested by Goldberg. In what ways are the responses of the woman different than the male responses?

4. Discuss why there are such differences.

5. Review the Scripture in Genesis. Can you see other reasons why Cain might have been filled with rage? What might you have counseled if given the opportunity?

"What mighty ills have not been done by woman! Who wasn't betrayed the Capital-A woman! Who lost Mark Antony the world? -A Woman! Who was the cause of a long ten years' war, and laid at last old Troy in Ashes? - Woman! Destructive, damnable, deceitful woman!"

Thomas Otway, The Orphan, Act III se i

Stress: "Any interference which disturbs the function of the organism at any level, and which produces a situation which is natural for the organism to avoid."
L. Howard
Stress defined: *"a non-specific response of the body to any demand, whether it is caused by or results in, pleasant or unpleasant conditions."*
Hans Selye.

Chapter 3
Family Stress and Distress

To my great dismay as a counselor and pastor, I have heard such sentiments even form Christian men as expressed by the quote on the previous page. For many men in our Western culture, all stress and distress can be traced to the wife of their youth. This projection of blame for the stress in the family is one of the key ingredients in dysfunctional and acting out behavior.

Another key reason found for the acting out of anger or rage in the home is the accumulation of unresolved stress in the family. Selye defines stress as a "non-specific response of the body to any demand, whether it is caused by or results in, pleasant or unpleasant conditions" (Selye. 1956, p. 74).

The principle cause of most health problems, and unhealthy family systems, is stress. Dr. William F. Lee has stated "Science...cannot alleviate the causes (of stress and distress), they can only control the symptoms. The only cure for stress comes from a reawakening of our relationship with God..." (Lee, 1989. pp. 8-9).

Some would look at Lee's statement with resolute dismay at its simplicity. Others would embrace it wholeheartedly. Even in our secular society "spiritual" answers to the distress of modern living are being sought. The 12-step movement, New Age philosophy and techniques, and humanistic psychology all look for a spiritual dimension as at least a component of the distressing of society. They look, unfortunately, to the wrong "spirit."

Stress, especially stress in the family is as old as mankind. One can easily see the dynamic tension in the relationship between Adam and Eve (especially after the fall), Cain and Abel (as previously discussed), Jacob and Esau, Moses with Pharaoh, Jesus in the garden, and Paul with the Judaizers. Stress is an inevitable aspect of living in our world. Distress, however, isn't an optional state, clearly beneath the level of comfort the Lord has promised for His people (peace or shalom).

The Causes

Family stress has been well documented over the years. Many causes can be named, including world industrialization, increase in family expectations, media, values changes, drugs and alcohol, poverty and racism, etc. Most families develop coping mechanisms that assist them in managing their stress and maintaining a fairly happy equilibrium. However, a growing percentage of families succumb to violence, sexual abuse or emotional outbursts to cope with the stress and distress of life.

Teaching couples involved in domestic violence how to manage stress and anger are keys to the treatment process. There are several ways in which stress gone out of control can manifest itself. These include:

Anger: Ephesians 4:26-27 states, "Be angry and yet do not sin. Do not let the sun go down on your anger, and do not give the devil an opportunity." It is not anger itself that is the problem, but unresolved anger that creates havoc, spiritually, emotionally, relationally and physically. Literally, anger can cause physical damage to the individual who displaces, projects, or represses feelings of rage. The over expression or the denial of anger can cause harm.

Managing Anger: Dr. Lee describes four steps in learning to manage anger. They include:

1. Teach the counselee to recognize anger. A lack of awareness or denial can suppress or repress anger, and as it were, lock it into place. Most men and women with problems managing anger are unaware of it until after the fact. A key to the treatment of stress and violence is teaching how to discern anger and deal with it differently.
2. Evaluate the causes of the anger, tracing its origin, function and triggers. This of course takes time, and is predicated on the individuals' willingness to admit that anger is a real problem.
3. Learn to positively control these energies through socially appropriate outlets such as journal writing or time out.
4. Confront the client's residual anger, learning to forgive and release bitterness and accept ourselves as created in God's image (Lee, 1989. pp. 32-33).

Guilt and Fear: Many times, like when a child is caught with his hand in the cookie jar, anger can be a response to guilt or fear. Guilt for being caught or shamed, fears of being abandoned or rejected, can create sufficient stress to develop emotional symptoms. Further, guilt or fear from past traumatic events or the discovery of those events, can create a similar response.

The Response: Most people respond to distress in the family by collapsing together in support. However, too often the response is the expression of stress in anger, co-dependency or sexual acting out. Many additional physical and emotional symptoms can also develop but are beyond the scope of this study.

Reducing Stress: There are several things that can be done to reduce the amount and type of stress that one experiences. According to Lee "One way (to manage stress) is called the **content of stress management.** Another way is called the **concept of stress management.**" By content of stress, Lee meant such things as nutrition, exercise, and relaxation. The concept of stress management deals with the following question: What can you do when there are limited choices? How can you cope with different personalities? How can you function when your self-image is low? How can you get into a power position when you feel powerless?

It may be helpful at this point to review some of the more common recognized stress producing situations. One such area is the gender reversal role. Stress increases when a female finds herself in a male dominated job or role and vice versa. Other factors causing stress include sicknesses, job change, change in environment, and perception.

A problem develops when the counselee does not own up to his or her problem and is incapable of hearing the fact that a problem actually exists. Lee suggests that "it is as though he is asleep."

The role of Christian counseling is to help the counselee wake up and make new and more appropriate decisions. People with low self-esteem make hasty or incorrect decisions because their creative and combative energies are low. People tend to look for other jobs and places to relocate when their sense of self-worth is diminished. They write resumes when their self-esteem is low and expect people to buy a product, namely themselves, when they do not believe in themselves. "Decisions made when there is a poor self-image result in an inadequate outcome," according to Lee.

To raise self-esteem requires realism and patience. In answer to the question, "What one thing can I do right now to help my self-image?" Lee suggests that the client needs to identify primary values and support those values behaviorally. Support-action is supporting behavior. When the client supports his family, children, job, church, etc., giving them the time and space they deserve, he is exhibiting supporting action. Once a value is identified it calls for action on the part of the person who has identified that value.

Lee suggests that, "Although content stress management experiences like exercise, nutrition, relaxation, etc., help cope with stress, there may be a value (concept) that has not been addressed properly which produces conflict.

The counselor needs to have the client make a list of things he values. Once the list is made, have the counselee prioritize that list, circling the things he values the most. Next would come the question, "What do you give most of your energy to?" What we give our energy and attention to is generally what we truly value.

Another major suggestion by Lee is that the client not let **others control their values** – which is another major cause of stress. Instead of allowing others in the environment to control our actions, we must learn to activate control over things we can control.

Activating Control is a very important tool for stress management. Lee postulates that "quality time together" may save a marriage that is on the verge of breaking up. The same principle applies to children who may be exhibiting the symptoms of stress or distress.

Another example of activating control is the avoidance or reduction of communication that may be causing the marriage to shift into a hostile mode. Lee suggests the use of a **conflict notebook** to keep a record of the types of situations that result in family conflict (or conflict with children, friends, etc.) so that the individual(s) may be able to take active control of those situations and practice avoiding them.

Stress Balance: As noted before, stress is not all bad. The absence of all stress is an undesirable state called death! Stress is that energy that pushes us forward or which can destroy us depending on how it is used and perceived. The object is to maintain flexible balance. In order to maintain this flexible balance it is important to have support systems. One type of support system is conditional. A conditional support system may be a job or may be relationships or even friendships. Another type of support system is the unconditional support system that allows positive self regard without specific ties or conditions. Faith in God through Jesus Christ is one example of an unconditional support system. Special interests such as hobbies, etc., also provide additional support if maintained in balance.

Effective Stress Counseling

Lee quotes Dr. Gary Collins, who in his book *Spotlight on Stress,* lists areas of pressure that cause stress. His Life Stages in the Life of Jesus found in the New Testament suggest some typological areas of stress that can disrupt family life.

Jesus' stress began when the angel Gabriel first visited Mary with the announcement of the events that were to follow. Joseph must have experienced considerable stress upon learning that his beloved, Mary, was with child before they were officially married. Some other examples listed by Collins include:

- The trip to Bethlehem where a stable became the birthplace of Christ (Luke 2:1-7).
- Herod's attempt to kill Jesus and the resulting massacre of all male children two years of age and younger (Matt. 2:16).
- The day Jesus stayed behind at the temple in Jerusalem and taught in the temple, no doubt causing great stress to His mother and father (let alone to the Pharisees, Luke 2:41-49).
- The wilderness experience, which must have caused a great deal of concern for His family (Luke 4:1-13).
- His radical teachings in the synagogue which caused people to run him out of town (Luke 4:30).
- Local opinion, as expressed by Nathaniel, "Can any good come out of Nazareth?" (John 1:46).
- The request of Mary at Cana to turn the water into wine (John 2:4).
- Jesus' rejection at Nazareth as being just a carpenter's son (Matt. 13:53-8).
- Gethsemane and the Cross of Calvary.

The final conclusion is that "Life is change and change is

stress."

Lee concludes that the how of coping with stress in the various stages varies greatly. The need is to become aware that stress exists in each phase of life. This alone is a beginning.

Stages of Possible Stressors

EARLY CHILDHOOD

leaving the womb
adjusting to light, temperature, touch, smell, etc.
communication, talking, eating
stages of walking
conscience and choice

MIDDLE CHILDHOOD

skills needed for simple games
developing the 3 R's
social interaction
developing morals and mores
self-esteem and independence
male/female relationships

ADOLESCENCE

independence of parents
sexual adaptability
academic & occupational goals
preparing for marriage and family
religious choice & maturation
social skills

EARLY ADULTHOOD

initiate occupational goals
reside away from home
marriage and children
proper social grouping
major purchases (car, house)
military obligations

MIDDLE ADULTHOOD

adjusting to vocational success
accepting economic status
encouraging & assisting children
adapting to physiological changes
relating to spouse as a person
develop leisure-time activities
responsibilities

LATER ADULTHOOD

reduced income, retirement
declining health and strength
death of spouse and peers
children's independence
grandparenting
social and civic
adjusting to living

> arrangements
> preparing for death

The reduction of stress begins with an adequate understanding of what stress is and what causes stress (and distress) at the various stages of life.

Jesus said, "But seek first his kingdom and his righteousness, and all of these things will be added to you." (Matt. 6:33). Ultimately, God's word provides many answers for the stress of life, but the avoidance of stress and distress is impossible. Learning to manage stress is essential to productive living in work and home.

For Class Discussion

1. Discuss Selye's definition of stress. What is considered as some of the causes of stress in humans?

2. Discuss the role of the Christian Counselor in dealing with people under stress.

3. Discuss self-esteem and tell how it can be raised.

4. Discuss Collins' stages of possible stressors.

"When angry, count to ten before you speak; if very angry, an hundred"

Thomas Jefferson, A Decalogue of Canons for Observation in Practical life

"Therefore be imitators of God, as beloved children; and walk in love, just as Christ also loved you and gave Himself up for us, an offering and a sacrifice to God as a fragrant aroma…and be subject to one another in the fear of Christ."

Ephesians 5:1-2, 21

People love to talk but hate to listen. Listening is not merely not talking. Though even that is beyond most of our powers; it means taking a vigorous, human interest in what is being told us. You can listen like a blank wall or like a splendid auditorium where every sound comes back fuller and richer.
Alice Duer Miller

Chapter 4
Family Communication and Violence

Healthy communication is a necessary ingredient for success, happiness, and contentment. God created us with the desire and need for intimate communication with the Lord and with one another.

In families where domestic violence is demonstrated, communication is often difficult, skewed, dysfunctional, or non-existent. For healthy families to grow, healthy communications that are positive and esteem enhancing are required. For unhealthy, dysfunctional families to maintain their dysfunction, unhealthy communication patterns must be established and maintained. As a Christian counselor, you will find that most families of domestic violence have extremely faulty communication.

Roadblocks to Communication in the Family

There are several areas in which communication can be difficult. Some have been described in Dr. William Carter's book, *Family Communication*. One roadblock is **"right words at the wrong time."** In communication, as in many areas of life, trivia is everything. In violent or abusive family systems, the wrong word seems to be spoken at the wrong time, and the right word at the wrong time. Because of the defensive and vulnerable state of the family, members generally are unclear in their communication and rarely is helpful communication presented.

Secondly, **overstatement of a valid point** can cause communication blocks. Some would call this form of communication nagging or badgering. Rather than clearly stating a point, dysfunctional families will overstate their position until they receive an unconscious, yet predetermined, response, whether withdrawal, aggression, or whining, the self-fulfilling prophecy of the others' response is fulfilled. Lectures and sermons are frequently said, but rarely heard in violent family systems. Members of violent families learn to tune out early in life to avoid the unpleasant lecture. Often resentment builds, setting the stage for emotional/physical outbursts.

Other roadblocks of significance include **mind reading** (always predicting what the family member will say or do), **finger pointing**, **constantly projecting blame** and accusing the other for family problems, and **gossip**, where nothing is truly confidential. This is part of the family betrayal, and often is a part of a triangulation of communication between mom, dad and one or more siblings. For more information on communication in the family, the reader is referred to Dr. DeKoven's book Marriage and Family Life: A Christian Perspective.

The Results. As one can imagine, the results of faulty communication are broken or damaged relationships. Lack of understanding leads to confusion, mistrust, fear, and even violence. The importance of clear communication modeled by the Christian counselor is most important. Much more will be said on this in the chapters on treatment.

The Bible and Communication

The Word of God speaks volumes on this most vital topic. However, the Apostle Paul speaks most profoundly on the importance of godly communication, as found in the book of Ephesians 4:25-32; it reads:

"Therefore, laying aside falsehood, SPEAK TRUTH EACH ONE of you WITH HIS NEIGHBOR, for we are members of one another. BE ANGRY, AND yet DO NOT SIN; Do not let the sun go down on your anger, and do not give the devil an opportunity. He who steals must steal no longer; but rather he must labor, performing with his own hands what is good, so that he will have something to share with one who has need. Let no unwholesome word proceed from your mouth, but only such a word as is good for edification according to the need of the moment, so that it will give grace to those who hear. Do not grieve the Holy Spirit of God, by whom you were sealed for the day of redemption. Let all bitterness and wrath and anger and clamor and slander be put away from you, along with all malice. Be kind to one another, tender-hearted, forgiving each other, just as God in Christ also has forgiven you."

Honest, loving and clear communication is lacking in the violent family system. But with the grace and mercy of God and judicious application of God's Word, positive, Godly communication can be developed.

For Class Discussion

1. Discuss the various roadblocks to communication in the family.

2. Discuss what the Bible has to say about communication.

3. Make a list of scriptures that refer to good or bad communication.

"The man that lays his hand upon a woman,
save in the way of kindness,
is a wretch whom't were gross flattery
to name a coward"

John Tobin, The Honeymoon, II

*A constant dripping on a day of steady rain
And a contentious woman are alike;*
Proverbs 27:15
*It is better to live in a corner of a roof
Than in a house shared with a contentious woman.*
Proverbs 21:9
*It is better to live in a desert land
Than with a contentious and vexing woman.*
Proverbs 21:19

Chapter 5
Spousal Abuse:
Dynamics of Rage

Spousal abuse usually involves abuse of the wife, but more and more frequently the husband may be the victim. Spousal abuse has reached epidemic proportions in western cultures. It has long been a very real problem in other parts of the world. The national pastime of "bashing" one's spouse is definitely on the increase. Spousal abuse, or marital violence, occurs in all segments of society, including the church (Brewer, 1990).

Marital violence can be defined as any physical, emotional, sexual, economic or verbal violence or abuse which is ongoing and persistent, causing severe distress to one spouse or the other. Battering or abuse creates a pattern of learned helplessness, a feeling of worthlessness and hopelessness, and intense fear.

Marital Violence, as defined by Brewer, can be expressed as follows:

1. **Incidents:** It is estimated that 1 out of 10 women are battered each year in Western nations. Spouse battering is the nation's most unreported crime -- less reported than rape. The more it happens the more likely it is to happen again. Battering can take three forms of

Patterns of Destruction

expression, which include: physical abuse, psychological/emotional abuse, and sexual abuse. Each is discussed in detail here.

2. **Physical violence** includes any act or behavior that inflicts bodily harm. Major physical assaults can include:

   Slaps and punches to the face and head
   Kicking, stomping and punching all over the body
   Choking to the point of unconsciousness.
   Pushing or throwing her across the room or down stairs.
   Severe shaking.
   Arms bruised or broken.
   Burns from irons or cigarettes.
   Broken ribs and arms resulting from woman raising her arms to protect herself.

3. In addition to physical abuse there is the problem of **psychological/emotional abuse.** This type of abuse consists of overt and veiled threats of violence as well as the consistent tearing down and ridicule of a spouse's character. This form of abuse has the effect of lowering one's self-esteem and leads to a feeling of learned helplessness. These threats of violence can include:

   a. Verbal expressions of intent to inflict bodily harm.
   b. Threatening gestures.
   c. Injury to pets.
   d. Destruction of property.
   e. Wielding of weapons.
   f. Any other intimidating verbal or non-verbal behavior.

Verbal and emotional abuse often leads to physical abuse, but even without an act of physical injury, the potential damage to the victim can be devastating. It should be noted that there is seldom only one victim with either physical or emotional abuse.

More often than not, children suffer as victims of the psychological/emotional abuse that is directed against a spouse. Brewer also noted that "threats of violence may be <u>more</u> damaging than the violent act itself."

An equally sinister form of abuse is that of **isolation.** Here the spouse may be kept from any contact with anyone except the abuser. The abuser works at weaning the spouse away from everyone that might take away attention from the abuser. He may intercept her mail, spy on her, and/or demand a complete accounting of time.

Further, abuse can take the form of **humiliation and degradation** once the victim spouse is isolated. The key communication given is that no one would care for or even want the victimized spouse.

The enforcement of trivial demands can be extremely abusive behavior. The abuser insists on compliance with trivial demands such as food, household arrangements, clothing, children, money and conversation.

In this form of abuse the victim spends enormous energy focusing on the demands of the abuser in fear of the potential rage that may result. Everything becomes important in terms of how it will affect the abuser.

Co-dependency, similar to that of alcoholism, thus develops, entrenching the victim.

4. Often wives that are abused physically are also victims of **sexual abuse.** Sexual abuse may take the form of **marital rape** in which the unwilling partner is forced to participate in intercourse or other sexual acts against his/her will.

Marital rape can also involve forced sex in front of children, forced sex during sickness, forced sex after a beating, but always involves a total disregard for the spouse's self-esteem and sexuality. The abused spouse becomes a sex object. The abuser constantly minimizes the importance of the spouse's feeling about sex and criticizes her/his sexuality. Often sexual abuse involves the calling of names (whore, frigid, impotent, etc.).

Sexual abuse often includes some forms of sexual perversity.

Most sexual abuse is committed at home involving the perpetrator (usually the husband) and the spouse and often takes place in the kitchen, the bedroom or the living room. Usually this form of abuse takes place in the evening on a weekend. High stress and arguments often precede it. Most incidents occur in a cycle, best described in a book by Lenore Walker (Walker, 1979.) and include:

1. **Tension Building**: This phase is evidenced by mounting stresses and tension, gradual escalation of incidents and irritation over things like finances and/or children. Some expressions of dissatisfaction are present, but not often dealt with directly. Feelings are repressed, becoming more and more intense. Communication and cooperation diminish. Dissatisfaction and hostilities build and a minor battering incident occurs. At this level the spouse attempts to rationalize their behavior.

Strangely enough, the wife often identifies with the batterer's faulty reasoning. She may try to placate the husband, attempting not to respond to his hostile action. Tension increases as the wife finds she is unable to control her husband's angry responses.

This is the point where the **"Learned Helplessness"** syndrome sets in, leaving the victim the feeling of powerlessness to prevent the cycle of violence or abuse from happening. Every move the victim makes is subject to misinterpretation, and the wife usually withdraws in order to avoid making things worse.

The husband, seeing the spouse's withdrawal, reacts with more intense anger. Tension becomes unbearable, and the wife may at this point precipitate or bring on the inevitable explosion so that she can minimize the pain or injury.

Alcohol often is a part of the violent episode. This entire episode may last from one hour to several months.

2. **Violent Episodes.** The uncontrollable tensions that have built up in the first phase of the violence scenario will usually erupt in what Walker has called "Violent Episodes." The anticipation of what may occur creates severe psychological stress for the battered spouse. Prior to the actual violent outburst there often exists a feeling that the outburst is inevitable. The batterer unleashes his aggression toward the wife (or husband).

During the abuse, the woman may psychologically disassociate her mind from her body in an effort to cope with the pain. However, there is a complete lack of predictability and control during this cycle.

Just before the violence occurs, the perpetrator may withdraw and not communicate because of a feeling of inability to compete with the spouse's verbal arguments. This withdrawal results in a heightened frustration. The withdrawal is a signal to the spouse that he is about to lose control in the relationship, and thus potentially suffer loss.

After the abuse the husband and wife both feel victimized. Though not all violence will follow this precise cycle (for instance, it is also true that many acts of violence are not preceded by any verbal arguments, but are based totally on impulse) this is the general cycle. This phase can last from a few minutes to 24-48 hours.

3. The final phase discussed by Walker is the **Honeymoon Phase.** It is the period immediately following the second phase and usually brings a period of almost blissful calm. Tensions have been dissipated for the moment. There are usually apologies by the abusing spouse, and some acts of extreme kindness may be shown.

The husband may beg for forgiveness, promising to never let the abuse happen again. His behavior may resemble that of a little boy caught in a transgression. It must be noted that the confession and subsequent request for forgiveness are rather shallow, although the victimizer may genuinely believe that he will not repeat the action and never allow himself to become violent again.

The battered wife may desire to leave her abusive husband, but often is dissuaded from leaving by relatives and friends of the husband or even an unsuspecting pastor, whom he has engaged to plead his cause. Guilt and a sincere desire to believe that things will be better may bring a decision by the wife to stay on with an abusive husband.

The remorseful attitude of the husband and the subsequent lavishing of kindness may cause the battered wife to catch a glimpse of the original dream of true love. All of this causes her to stay in the abusive relationship.

During the make-up part of this phase it is often reported that the couple has achieved a level of intimacy that is at the best in the lives of the couple. The wife tends to believe that the behavior that she sees in her husband during the honeymoon stage is evident of what her husband is really like. She begins to believe that she can be the source of healing for her husband. During this period of relative bliss, the battered wife finds it difficult to even think about leaving her husband.

There is a temporary shift of power in the relationship, with the wife feeling that she is in fact in control. Over time, the honeymoon cycle will come to an end, and without intervention, the balance of power will shift again. The honeymoon periods become shorter and shorter with each violent incident, and the violence increases without intervention.

Forces Against Change

According to Geller (1992), there are five primary forces against changing the violent family dance. They include:

1. **Conspiracy of Silence** - Since no one in the family desires exposure due to shame and fear, an unconscious code or conspiracy of silence exists. Though everyone wants the violence to stop, there is a dread of confrontation and exposure, two necessary components of change. Little real healing can occur in any area of life as long as it remains in darkness.
2. **Societal attitudes**- which include such beliefs as "adults make their own choices," women are blamed for staying in the relationship, and the Judeo-Christian ethic prohibiting divorce as well as the concept that you "reap what you sow" can limit the perceived choices of men and women.
3. **Clergy non-support** - teaching that one should stay for the sake of the children. 21% of clergy state that no amount of abuse warrants leaving a husband. However, the majority felt it was appropriate or permissible to separate if the abuse was "severe" (undefined). The teaching on submission was cited as the primary reason to endure. In light of the reality of the co-abuse of the children in the home, this hardly seems wise.
4. **Substance abuse** - which, as will be discussed in greater detail later, is often a major contributor to abusive episodes.
5. **Women stay due to financial pressures** -- they often feel trapped and helpless, without the personal empowerment to act.

The very concept of spousal abuse is abhorrent to a large segment of our culture. To hit or otherwise abuse a woman or child seems beyond the imagination of most Christian people. Yet it does exist, and must be dealt with seriously. In Malachi 3: 10-14, the prophet of God speaks the Lord's heart as related to family life and especially the treatment of a man for his wife. Marriage is a covenant for life from God's perspective. Yet, as seen in this passage, the men in Israel were abusing their wives and sending them away in divorce for virtually any reason. The Lord called this treachery. Abuse of a spouse, whether verbal, physical or sexual cannot be tolerated, laughed at, winked at or otherwise minimized. It is a horrible blight on a civilized culture, and must be dealt with.

For Class Discussion

1. Discuss the issue of spousal abuse. What are some of the ways spousal abuse can be included as forms of spousal abuse? Are there other forms of spousal abuse that you would add to the list?

2. Discuss the subject of co-dependency.

3. Discuss the subject of marital rape, its causes and the legal and ethical ramifications.

4. Discuss the phases of spousal abuse as presented by Walker.

5. Review Malachi 3 and find a parallel passage which condemn violence towards women in general or specific.

" My wife nagged me so much that I couldn't take it any more. I met some of my mates at the local pub, and we began to knock down a few. The more I talked about my nagging wife, the more my friends encouraged me to set her in her place. So I bashed her up! You can't blame me for it, I can't even remember it!" An interview with an abusive husband.

"They struck me, but I did not become ill; They beat me, but I did not know it. When shall I awake? I will seek another drink."

Proverbs 23:35

Jellinek's Disease (alcoholism) is responsible for:
50 percent of all auto accidents
80 percent of all home violence
30 percent of all suicides
60 percent of all child abuse
65 percent of all drownings
It is estimated that when a woman contracts the disease, her husband leaves her in nine out of ten cases; when a man contracts it, his wife leaves in one out of ten cases.
Kathleen Whalen Fitzgerald

Chapter 6
Alcohol/Drugs and Abuse

Much has been written on the devastating effect that substance abuse (alcohol and illegal drugs) has had on western society. I will not attempt to develop this theme too deeply.

In the Baker Encyclopedia of Psychology, Baker Book, 1985, T.M Johnson states that "a substance is defined as any chemical that modifies mood or behavior by affecting the central nervous system and whose use is subject to misuse. Such a definition obviously excludes the use of medications when they are used as prescribed. Pathological use of substances may include legal drugs (such as caffeine) of illegal drugs (such as cocaine). A substance-use disorder is characterized by maladaptive behavior associated with the use of substances." (pg 1128)

Increasing evidence points to a significant correlation between alcohol abuse and domestic violence (including sexual abuse). Alcohol is a central nervous system depressant, creating symptoms of a lack of social inhibition, poorer than normal impulse control, feelings of euphoria, lessened coordination, and impaired judgment. This, added to severe mental distress, financial pressure, etc., can set the stage for acting out behavior. Alcohol and drug abuse are not causative factors in violent/abusive behavior, but frequently the abuse of alcohol and/or drugs can be the catalyst for violence. Anger and hostility, as well as immature attempts at sexual/emotional fulfillment are generated by communication between couples and other family members, not directly by the intake of alcohol.

Obviously, as Christians, no substance should control our lives. We have been bought with a price (I Corinthians 6:20). We are to yield our bodies as instruments of righteousness, not allowing ourselves to become overcome by the abuse of substances. Though substance abuse is not to be a part of the life of a Christian, it certainly can and does. As a Christian counselor, it is essential to look for alcohol or other substance abuse where violent behaviors are manifested in the family system. In review, alcohol/drugs will:

1. **Lower good judgment-** The use of alcohol will reduce the individuals ability to know their own strength or show necessary restraint if an argument ensues. This lowered judgment leads to "accidents" between couples in the home.
2. **Decrease inhibitions-** the person under the influence of alcohol or drugs can become bold in their assertions. The substance "gives permission" for the intoxicated person to say what ever comes to mind and do whatever tickles their fancy. This lack of social restraint can lead to all sorts of acting out behavior, including violence. Essentially, the drugs or alcohol give "permission" to impulsive feelings of rage and hostility, as well as to sexual/emotional acting out.

Where present, alcohol/drug dependency must be treated as part of the intervention in the family. " The traditional individual psychotherapeutic interventions have not been very successful with substance-abuse problems". (ibid, pg 1130) Treatment can best be done in either an inpatient setting, such as a hospital or residential treatment setting, and or in a combined AA/NA program with individual and family therapy. It is important to remember, however, that a "dry" alcoholic is not necessarily sober (defined as being in ones clear thinking or right mind). They can often express repressed hostility even more when dry, since alcohol/drug consumption was often used as a stress reducer or conflict avoider. In either case, alcohol/substance abuse must be evaluated and often treated as part of the treatment strategy for violence in the family. When present, it is not the cause of the abuse in he family, but is often the lubricant used by the abuser to grease the skids towards abusive behavior.

For Class Discussion

1. Discuss the problem of alcohol and drug abuse in relationship to family violence.

2. What are some of the evidences of alcohol or drug abuse?

When a teenager gets to age 13, the best way to deal with them is to put them into a box, close the lid and feed them through a hole left in the top. Then, when they turn 16, plug the hole!

A paraphrase of the story told by Mark Twain

*Nothing has a stronger influence psychologically
on their environment, and especially on their children,
than the unlived lives of the parent.*
Carl Jung
*Adolescents will tend to treat their younger siblings and
their parents in the same way that they were treated by
their parents throughout their lives.*
JJB

Chapter 7
Adolescent Violence in the Family

Most of us in the United States were shocked as we watched the burning, looting and violence demonstrated in the infamous Rodney King/L.A. riots. Men and women destroyed property, caused bodily harm, looted and pillaged in response to perceived injustice and a repressive society. Years of frustration, suspicion and hatred erupted, spreading to other cities across our land.

As I watched the riots from afar (while praying for many of my friends and neighbors in L.A.), I couldn't help but see the intense expression of rage coming through the adolescents and pre-adolescents of the community at large. This is but a microcosm of the battles occurring in families daily, even in Christian homes.

Now, lest I become too cynical, in defense, adolescence is not a disease (though many parents believe they may die from it). Most teenagers not only survive, but also thrive during the years of identity formation, hormones and zits. But for too many, family stress leads to family violence perpetrated against parents and younger siblings.

Abuse by Adolescents

What are some of the causes of abuse by adolescents and

how can it be handled?

1. **Family problems**. Adolescents are caught in a unique struggle. They are neither child nor adult. They carry some of both, the naiveté of childhood with the inherent needs, and the power (both physical and emotional) of an adult. As children grow into adulthood, especially if they have been overly coerced or abused, or have observed abuse as a resolution to stress or family problems, they will likely repeat the patterns in their family and the community at large. There are certain names that have been given to the roles that people will play in order to attempt to resolve the problems inherent in an abusive family. Dr. Virginia Satir, a well-known psychotherapist and educator has elucidated the roles that adolescents might play. They include:

    a. **The enabler.** Often the spouse or parent, though it can be one of the other children, the enabler is usually the one the abuser depends upon the most. This family member becomes more and more responsible for the family to make up for the lack of control of the abuser or the lack of input into the family.
    b. **The family hero.** This individual is especially sensitive to the family's needs. They feel responsible for its pain. The hero does everything possible to improve the situation by trying to present him or herself as a success in the environment outside the home.
    c. **The scapegoat.** The scapegoat does not work as hard as the hero to achieve recognition, but instead, pulls away in a destructive manner by getting into trouble, hurting themselves or withdrawing. In doing this they attempt to bring the attention of the

family away from the abuser and onto themselves.
d. **The lost child.** This child offers relief to the family by taking care of personal problems and avoiding trouble. The family ignores the child who is then left to face problems all alone. In many cases, this child is the one who suffers the most pain within the family while seeming to be the least affected.
e. **The mascot.** This person provides relief for the family through humor. By being the "class clown" they mask their own pain and loneliness for the sake of what seems to be the good of the family.

In each case, the adolescent may, under the right circumstances, explode out of their dysfunctional role, often violently, in an attempt to seek relief or help in the family.

What intervention can assist the family with an acting out adolescent, and further assist the family? First, there is...

a. **Intervention,** which is designed to motivate the abuser to seek help. Without help, whether through intervention by the Spirit of God by a tremendous conversion experience, or through the loving support of a family, the abuser is likely to continue to abuse as a way to meet their desperate needs. Thus, intervention is often a first step in an overall treatment process.
b. **Treatment.** Without exception, Christ-centered treatment of the abuser and the victim is needed. An abusive adolescent will become an abusive adult. I have said many times, "The most normalized, well integrated human being that does not know Christ, is just as readily going to hell as one that is a total mess." With that in mind, I believe it is essential for an abuser to come to

know Christ as their personal savior. Having the Holy Spirit living within their hearts is an important first step if they are going to be able to overcome the temptations of the devil and to be able to walk in victory over their abusive patterns.

c. **Re-socialization**- Along with intervention and treatment (generally outpatient, though some will require more intensive, inpatient programs) most abusers, especially teenagers, must learn how to re-socialize themselves. In most cases, they have had very little or poor parenting. They need to re-learn how to live and solve problems in a more appropriate manner. This is where 12-step groups, such as developed by Alcoholics Anonymous (preferably from a Christian perspective), in conjunction with supportive counseling services, will help to re-integrate the individual abuser while teaching them to live a Christian life.

d. **Living the Word-**There is certainly no substitute for learning the Word of God and how to apply the word to their lives. In most cases, they will need a strict and disciplined approach because they have learned to survived in a very dysfunctional, undisciplined and very self-absorbed manner. The counselor involved with an abuser must be wary and use wisdom in ministering to them.

For Class Discussion

1. What are some of the causes of adolescent abuse in the family?

2. Discuss the various names of the roles that Satir has given to individuals in the family.

3. Discuss the possible interventions that can assist the family.

"And they were bringing even their babies to Him so that He would touch them, but when the disciples saw it, they began rebuking them. But Jesus called for them, saying, 'Permit the children to come to Me, and do not hinder them, for the kingdom of God belongs to such as these.' 'Truly I say to you, whoever does not receive the kingdom of God like a child will not enter it at all.'"

"But whoever causes one of these little ones who believe in Me to stumble, it would be better for him to have a heavy millstone hung around his neck, and to be drowned in the depth of the sea."

Jesus, Luke 18:15-17, Matthew 18:6

Children, obey your parents in the Lord, for this is right.
HONOR YOUR FATHER AND MOTHER (which is the first commandment with a promise),
SO THAT IT MAY BE WELL WITH YOU, AND THAT YOU MAY LIVE LONG ON THE EARTH.
4 Fathers, do not provoke your children to anger, but bring them up in the discipline and instruction of the Lord.
Ephesians 6:1-4

Chapter 8
Child Abuse

In answering the question "Why Child Abuse Happens," Blair Justice and Rita Justice state, "The vast majority of people who have physically abused children are not maniacs or even parents who do not love their children. As a group they defy psychiatric classification. They come from all socioeconomic groups and all educational levels" (in Justice and Justice.).

The question is, therefore, how then do they differ from parents who do not abuse their children?

Justice and Justice quote Gill as saying "...reports of child abuse were heavily concentrated among the poor. Child abuse, he suggested, may be regarded largely as being one more aspect of the poverty syndrome" (Gill. 1982).

A similar viewpoint is presented by Gelles' theory of child abuse. He saw child abuse as a particular form of adaptation to stress. He also considered such factors as societal values and norms, socialization experience, and "psychopathic states." But his theory mainly emphasizes such stress areas as a socioeconomic position of parents, marital stresses, excessive number of children, unemployment, social isolation, unwanted or "problem" children, and precipitating situations such as an argument or child misbehavior (Gelles. 1979).

Perhaps Kempe, Helfer, and their colleagues suggested the

foremost theory in the field of child abuse. This group of researchers presented a "three-factor" theory: First, the parents must have the potential to abuse, primarily as a result of receiving an inadequate "mothering imprint" in their own childhood. Second, the parent must see the child as being "special" or different, whether he or she really is or not. Third, a crisis must occur that triggers the abuse (Kempe. 1984)

Abusing parents have in their lives what Holmes and Rahe call a "chronic state of life crises" (Holmes and Rahe. 1979) Justice and Justice also suggest that in Selye's (Selye. 1979), three stages of responding to stress, no sooner had the abusive parents transversed the first phase of shock and countershock that they entered the second stage, that of resistance, when a new crisis came along, and they plunged into the third stage -- exhaustion. It is this stage of exhaustion, when defenses are lowest and controls on acting out behavior are weakest, that abuse occurs.

Helfer noted that "Most abusive parents are products of the 'World of Abnormal Rearing.' The cycle begins with parents having unrealistic expectations of their child" (Helfer. 1990).

It is an old story. The parents expect to receive nurturing from the child, and, although he may do the best he can, he never meets all of their expectations. In Ericksonian terms, the child never really learns **trust.** In this type of family situation the process becomes cyclical. Everyone wants love and nurturing from others who usually are simply not able to meet their expectations. The demand is just too heavy.

The child in the abusing situation is to be considered as a contributing factor. The parent's abuse is directed at a "special child" the one that the parents perceive as being most in need, or the child may be the one that is in the greatest competition to the parent seeking the same thing. At high risk of being physically abused are children who are premature, twins, retarded or handicapped, adopted, congenitally malformed, conceived during a mother's depressive illness, or children of mothers with frequent pregnancies.

A final factor suggested by Justice and Justice in the Psycho-social Stress Model is what they call "cultural scripts." By this they mean the accepted and expected patterns of interaction between individuals in a society.

The biblical "script" that is often quoted and misused is "Spare the rod and spoil the child," which does indeed reflect an attitude of violence toward the child. A clear understanding of the Biblical passages is necessary. Discipline is needed for children (the intent of the passages is not brutalization). Other cultural scripts include; "Madonna mother, Gerber baby, Super-moms" and others, usually the result of media presentation of the ideal. These cultural scripts serve as a source of frustration and feelings of guilt by potentially abusive parents and actually lead to more violence and abuse of children.

It should be noted that much of what has been said about the causes of the abuse of children could be also said about other types of abuse.

Types of Child Abuse

Child abuse can be seen as physical, emotional or sexual abuse or neglect perpetrated against a child in custodial care. There are several individuals or agencies that may come into play in dealing with child abuse or neglect. They include[2]:

Law Enforcement: By the very nature of their community role and their legal authority, the police and sheriff's departments are the principal agencies responding to family crisis situations. The responding officer will decide whether to take the child into protective custody (Welfare and Institutions Code Section 305, California), to arrest the parents/caretakers, to seek the filing of criminal charges or refer the case to another appropriate agency. In some law enforcement agencies, the child abuse units include

---

[2] The source of this information is taken from *Child Abuse Prevention Handbook*, presented by the State of California

full-time social service workers who respond to calls with the officers as an investigative team.

The investigating officer seeks answers to the following questions when determining whether child abuse actually occurred:

1. Is this an isolated incident, or is there a history of abuse, neglect or family disturbances? (Verification of prior reports can be made through record checks).
2. Is there a perceived danger to the child or other children in the home?
3. How was the incident reported? Who reported the alleged incident, if known?
4. What is the emotional and mental attitude of the parents?
5. What is the general condition of the home?
6. Are the nature and severity of injuries indicative of abuse or neglect?
7. What is the general behavior of the parents?
    - Are the explanations of the child's injuries inadequate?
    - Do the parents/caretakers vehemently place the blame upon others.
    - Are the parents/caretakers apathetic or insensitive to the child's condition?

Once the investigating officer is inside the home, he will isolate the child, and with sensitivity, question him or her as to the cause of the injuries. The officer will also examine the child thoroughly for discoverable injuries, such as broken limbs, cuts and bruises.

Depending on the age of the child, a visual examination of the child's anatomy should be conducted to ascertain the existence of burns on the buttocks or bottom of the feet or injuries to other areas hidden by clothes. Very often it is impossible for an officer or a lay person to detect an injury, for example, when the injury is not visible, as in the case of internal hemorrhaging. Head injuries are particularly dangerous and often detectable only by x-ray.

Therefore if an officer has any reason to suspect a head injury, the child should be taken to a medical facility for an examination. Additionally, a complete examination of all children in the family is advisable when child abuse is suspected.

If the preliminary investigation indicates abuse, the officer will take the child to a facility that has doctors trained to detect child abuse injuries. The child should be carefully and sensitively told where he/she is being taken, why this is being done, and what to expect.

The process of investigating shall continue as per standard procedures.

Legal Community: In addition to the adult court which handles the criminal cases of adult offenders, and the juvenile courts which make determinations about dependent children as previously discussed, the "legal community" is basically composed of three additional agencies: the county district attorney, the county counsel and the city attorney.

Depending on the county or jurisdiction, the judge, prosecutor and defense attorney may agree to defer prosecution if the suspect is receptive to psychotherapy, family counseling or other rehabilitative help; or they may prosecute and then agree to probation supervision.

Probation: When ordered to do so by the courts, the probation department investigates adult offenders convicted of child abuse or neglect. A court report outlining the offender's social history, prior record, offense and attitude is submitted. The report also evaluates suitability for probation and, in appropriate cases, recommends probation with specific conditions aimed at control and treatment, psychiatric or psychological treatment, family treatment and/or enrollment in self-help programs are typically recommended in these cases, along with the other standard conditions or probation.

In order to assure the child's safety and welfare, the supervising officer also works cooperatively with the protective services worker assigned to the case. Their assessment of the child's needs and the offender's response to treatment is of significant influence in determining when, and if, the child will be returned to the home.

Medical Community: Doctors, nurses, dentists and all other types of professional medical personnel play a crucial role in child abuse detection. In addition, other indices of abuse that hospitals and medical personnel should consider are:

- history of repeated injuries
- delays in seeking medical care
- discrepancies in explanations, history and the nature of injuries
- injuries not reported by parents and found in physical examination and X-ray.
- generally inadequate nutrition and poor health
- the child is extremely passive, compliant or fearful
- evidence of sexual activity or abuse
- bruises or broken bones in an infant or toddler
- x-rays showing chip or metaphysical fracture in joints (a result of twisted limbs)
- head injuries
- abdominal and/or internal injuries
- behavior of parents (overreact or under-react; cannot remember how it happened; insensitive to child's pain or condition; refuse consent for further examination of child; blame others; appear detached or apathetic)

Some in the medical community may think child abuse is a problem that does not warrant involving law enforcement. It should be emphasized that in almost all civilized nations the law requires doctors and nurses (and other mandated reporters previously listed) to report abuse to a child protective agency (the police or sheriff, county probation, or county welfare) if a suspicion of abuse is present.

Social Welfare: The importance of a county welfare (social services) department's role lies in both crisis intervention and the ongoing services it provides to children and families in difficulty.

County welfare department personnel provide immediate response to emergency situations on a 24-hour basis. Such crisis intervention generally involves short-term protective and social services for children and families. Workers utilize available community resources and coordinate case plans with other agencies to maximize services to the family.

When a child is declared a dependent of the court, social welfare agencies supervise the child for the court at home or in a placement, offer ongoing social services to the family and/or the child, including referral to needed treatment services, and make periodic progress reports to the court.

Schools: School teachers, nurses, counselors, principals and supervisors of child welfare and attendance and other designated school personnel who are mandated to report suspected child abuse cases play a critical role in the early detection of child abuse and neglect. Symptomatic signs of abuse and/or neglect, which may include injuries, listlessness, poor nutrition, disruptive behavior, absenteeism or depression, are often first seen by school personnel. Because immediate investigation of suspected abuse by proper child protective agencies may save a child from repeated injuries, school personnel should not hesitate to report suspicious injuries or behavior. Their duty is to **report,** not investigate.

Schools can also play a substantial role in the prevention of abuse and neglect by offering classes on marriage, parenting and child development to students. Parenthood education is vitally needed. We know that today's mistreated youth may be tomorrow's abusers unless interaction takes place. Classes in parenting through the schools may help break the pattern of successive generations of child abuse.

The Church: Often the church's role in dealing with child abuse is overlooked in literature on the subject. The church, however, has always offered many programs that can be of great influence in not only dealing with the problems of abuse among their own people, but by offering seminars and classes in family, parenting, personal, emotional restoration, etc. The church can be a great force in the prevention of future possible abuse.

Many churches are offering help in the way of a Family Care Center where free or very inexpensive counseling is offered to families and individuals of the congregation and other people from the community in general. This is a ministry that has long been needed. Some excellent training programs are being offered through such organizations as the Institute for Christian Counseling, which prepare lay workers for a ministry in counseling.[3]

---

[3] More information about a training program in Christian Counseling may be obtained by contacting Vision International University, www.vision.edu.

For Class Discussion

1. Discuss the subject of child abuse. Why do you think it occurs? To what extent does it exist in your community?

2. Discuss the types of questions that should be asked to determine if child abuse has actually occurred.

3. If you had to make a report of suspicion of Child abuse in your community, how is it to be done and to whom?

"I washed and washed, scrubbed and scrubbed for over 2 hours trying to get the filth of his body off of mine. No matter how hard I tried, I could never get clean. I feel so dirty, what can make me clean."

A wounded soul

To act without rapacity, to use knowledge without wisdom, to respect interdependence, to operate with our hubris and greed are not simply moral imperatives. They are an accurate scientific description of the means of survival.
Barbara Ward

Chapter 9
Sexual Abuse

Counseling a victim of sexual abuse, whether an incestuous relationship or perpetrated by a pedophile, is heart wrenching and sobering. To hear the story of a man or woman, even as adults, filled with the treachery and betrayal inherent in the abuse is heart breaking. As I write this section I am reminded of one of the earlier cases of child abuse I counseled.

Sharon (not her real name, but the story is true) was a 27 year old black woman from the inner city of Chicago, Ill. Her pastor referred her for counseling. Five years previous she had married a white man, and was very much in love. They had two beautiful children, and had weathered the racism of our society remarkably well. Since I knew Sharon from a distance through church, I was actually a bit surprised that she might need counseling. She presented as a highly competent (she was an attorney), intelligent and thoroughly delightful woman. However, she had a most insidious secret.

After the pleasantries of our initial session, Sharon in her normal bold and direct style began to relate her story. She had been raised in a single parent home with her mother and 6 siblings. Most of her brothers and sisters were the result of various liaisons that mom had had over the years. She was the oldest child, and the only man that her mother was married to was Sharon's father. However, she never knew her father.

She related that she had been suffering of late with bouts of depression and a general lack of desire for relations with her husband. Her husband, an engineer by trade had not complained much, and seemed by all accounts to be a loving gentleman. She just could not make herself interested in intimacy, and wondered why and why now.

The more we discussed her family and family of origin, the more clear the picture of her problems and their causes became. She related that her mother was not much of a caregiver, leaving the care of the children to her. Several times she remembers her mother bringing a man home who was not her or one of the other children's fathers. On one occasion, an incident occurred that altered her life and perception of relationships.

She related how she felt so very responsible for her younger siblings. When she was 13, one of her mother's boyfriends, drunk and out of control, attempted to sneak into her 11-year-old sisters room. His intentions were unclear, but she suspected that evening prayers were not on his mind. In an attempt to rescue her sister, she "invited" the man into her room, where she was repeatedly molested by the drunken slob of a man. His molestation of her continued for several months, only ending when in a drunken brawl he was kicked out of the house by her mother, never to be heard of again.

As she related her story, tears began to flow. She felt so terribly guilty for the "relationship", believing that it was her fault, that she should have done something to stop the man and protect not only her sister but also herself. Of course, she could not tell her mother for fear of mom's rejection and rage. Instead, like so many women, she buried her wound and suffered in silence, but the memories and shame would not go away.

Sharon's way of coping with the horror of her abuse was to compensate through overachieving in work and school. She made an internal vow that she would always protect her children, and also make sure that finances were strong to ensure she would never have to be dependent upon a man. Recently, she had changed her work to part-time to have more time with her own children, creating insecurity, but the trigger to her pain was seeing her husband, in a most appropriate way, giving loving affection to her daughter. Her fear that she could not protect her child from her husband or any other man had set her fear and the return of painful memories in motion. Thankfully, she was able to process through the grief of her lost innocence and develop a realistic perception of her abuse (it was not her fault), leading to a healthy resolution of her depression and pain.

Dr. Dan Allender writes in his excellent book, *The Wounded Heart*, "Sexual abuse often follows a typical sequence of stages. They are:

1) development of intimacy and secrecy;
2) enjoyment of physical touch that appears appropriate;
3) sexual abuse proper (physical contact or psychological interaction); and
4) Maintenance of the abuse and the shameful secret through threats and privileges" (Allender. 1990). Each are described briefly here.

Development of intimacy and secrecy. This is a conscious, deliberate set-up, seductive in nature, created by the perpetrator to victimize the child. The time frame for this set-up can be a day to years in process. The set-up may be very or mildly conscious. In Sharon's case, it was difficult to see any secret set-up. However, after some discussion she began to realize that the man who molested her had been flirting with her for some time, often right in from of her mother. She initially enjoyed the attention, as she had had very little father love in her upbringing. She had no idea what lurked in his mind, nor could she have anticipated his actions.

Enjoyment of physical touch that appears appropriate. This is the beginning of physical and sensual bonding between perpetrator and victim. This heightened relational intimacy is akin to love and meets a "need" in victim and victimizer. Areas of touching can include such things as hand holding, hugs, back rubs, etc., and to the neglected child is like a glass of water to a man lost in the desert. In Sharon's case, there was little more than verbal intimacy between them. However, she did relate how he would ask her to sit on his lap occasionally, and he would touch her hair in what felt a most affectionate way. The positive feeling of this limited affection felt genuine and pleasant to Sharon.

Sexual abuse proper (physical contact or psychological interaction. There are different levels and intensity of sexual abuse, and the extent of damage is not easily assessed. Dr. Allender states "Sexual abuse occurs in a context of loneliness, a context that set up the victim for a baffling interplay of betrayal and ambivalence, and powerlessness as the adult moves the victim from one stage of abuse to the next. Sexual abuse crosses the line between nurture and affection to relational sabotage" (Allender, 1990). This can include inappropriate manual or oral sexual arousal, sexual intercourse, or dialog of the same. The truth is that God made our bodies to respond to physical stimulation, creating obvious diabolical conflict (pleasure vs. pain). Even if the victim blocks feelings of arousal, sensations of pleasure occur each and every time. The mass of emotions triggered during sexual abuse creates nearly unending conflict, without treatment.

This was by far the most problematic part of the abuse Sharon experienced. The fact was, the abuse, as horrible and evil as it was, felt pleasurable. She could not justify in her mind the pleasure factor as being a natural bodily response, provided through adult sexual behavior far before her readiness for such behavior. It took many sessions of wrenching self-condemnation before she was able to receive the forgiveness of the Lord and acceptance of the truth of the molest.

Maintenance of the abuse and secrecy through threats and privileges. The perpetrator, fearing discovery and often desiring continuance of the relationship, will use fear (physical threats, exposure, and withdrawal of "attention") or use privileges (gifts, special status, etc.) to maintain the abuse and avoid discovery. This is why abuse can go on for years, undetected, without escape. For Sharon, it was the fear of discovery that maintained the abuse, as he threatened to kill her mother and molest her sister if she ever told what had happened between them.

Sexual Abuse Defined

Sexual abuse can take many forms. Sexual abuse can be defined broadly as "any sexual activity, verbal, visual, or physical, engaged in without consent, which may be emotionally or physically harmful and which exploits a person in order to meet another person's sexual or emotional needs" (McGee and Schaumburg. 1997).

Verbal sexual abuse consists of remarks including sexual threats, innuendoes, comments about a person's body, solicitation, harassment, coarse jesting, inappropriate sexual talking, and sexual name-calling.

Visual sexual abuse includes voyeurism, exhibitionism, viewing of pornographic material, or genitals, or of any sexual activity such as masturbation or intercourse.

Physical sexual abuse includes any inappropriate form of touching, from hugging to rape. Rubbing, holding, and kissing for the purpose of sexual gratification are examples. Also included in physical sexual abuse are oral, genital, anal and breast stimulation, and penetration by penis, fingers, or any other body part or object, of mouth, anus or vagina.

Ritualistic sex abuse represents the ultimate in human degradation, torture, mind control and destructiveness. The majority of such abusers are involved in satanic rituals and worship. The components of ritualistic abuse fall into four areas: physical, sexual, psychological, and spiritual. Though this form of abuse does exist, it appears that it does so to a very limited measure.

Information for Parents

Statistics will vary as to the frequency of child sexual abuse -- partially because it is estimated that only one in ten cases are reported, but estimates are that one in ten males are sexually abused and one in four females are abused. SOMEONE THEY KNOW, such as acquaintances, baby-sitters, friends of the family, or relatives abuses seventy-five percent of children.

Most children are tricked or manipulated, not forced into sexually abusive activity. Because bribery or threats are so often a part of the abuse, children may feel as if they are to blame. Sexual abuse is NEVER the victim's fault.

A person who commits a sexual offense needs outside intervention and help in order to stop his/her behavior. Keep in mind that it is the person's **behavior** that is wrong or bad, not the **person**. We do not do offenders any favors by not reporting them. In fact, most will never change their behavior unless caught and confronted. Also, the effectiveness of treatment of offenders often depends upon the type and extent of the abuse. Incest perpetrators tend to fair better in treatment, with good results if discovered early. However, with pedophiles, the average child molester has perpetrated against over 100 children prior to being caught, and the level of recidivism is extremely high, estimated by some at over 95%. Further, since most pedophiles believe that they were not hurting the children they were molesting, but actually loving them, treatment is a long and often ineffective process. Incarceration is often recommended for the protection of society.

Sexual abuse is a difficult, traumatic experience, yet there are many resources for victims, families and offenders. Not giving children information leaves them vulnerable in the future, as well as leading the child to believe that abusive activity is acceptable.

What to Let Children Know

Personal safety is as important as other safety rules we learn about. Determine what your children know about safety: what to do in case of fire, poisoning, how to cross the street, etc., and then let them know that personal body safety is important too!

Use the TOUCH Continuum as a tool to discuss different types of touch:

| **Lack of Touch** | **Good Touch** | **Confusing Touch** | **Bad Touch** |

Ask your children to discuss touch they think is good, such as games, hugs, kisses, etc. Then ask them what types of touch they think are bad, such a bullying, hitting, etc. Discuss the fact that there are times when touches may be confusing and they may not be sure if it is good or bad. It is also helpful to discuss any lack of touch and that some people do not touch much -- families and people are different in how much touching they do.

Stress that NO ONE, whether stranger, acquaintance, or relative, has the right to force or trick him or her into sexual contact or touch.

Develop your child's "support system" for help or information on this subject. The support system includes people they know like parent(s), relatives, friends, ministers, teachers and counselors. Other resources include places such as police department, child protective services, rape centers, mental health centers, etc.

Guides to Remember in Talking to Your Children

Listed here are three primary guidelines to remember when talking to your children.

1. Minimize the scariness of the conversation. Balance the conversation with issues of general safety.
2. Listen to your child's questions and responses. Do not attempt to tell them more than they can comprehend, and answer questions as honestly and straightforward as possible.

3. By talking, you are helping to prepare and protect your child. You are also taking a big step toward prevention of sexual abuse.
4. Always use a proper vocabulary.
5. Never laugh or joke about their questions or apparent ignorance, particularly in a serious conversation.

If You Suspect Your Child May Be a Victim

Even in the healthiest of parent/child relationships, children may be too embarrassed or scared to tell you what happened.

When your child reaches out for help, **LISTEN AND BE SUPPORTIVE**. A child may subtly hint at the incident, or a child's behavior may change. If you are angry or upset about what happened, let the child know that the anger is not toward him or her.

It is so very sad that we have to deal with topics such as sexual abuse in our society. Not only do parents need to educate their children, but churches need to educate the parishioners as well. Awareness of the problem is the first step to solving it. And all problems are best solved before they occur.

For Class Discussion

1. Discuss what constitutes sexual abuse, as suggested by Allender.

2. What is and is not to be thought of as sexual abuse?

3. What are some of the things that parents need to know about sexual abuse?

4. Discuss how much do children need to know about sexual abuse?

"Therefore, since we have a great high priest who has passed through the heavens, Jesus the Son of God, let us hold fast our confession. For we do not have a high priest who cannot sympathize with our weaknesses, but One who has been tempted in all things as we are, yet without sin. Therefore let us draw near with confidence to the throne of grace, so that we may receive mercy and find grace to help in time of need."

Hebrews 4:14-16

"And one will say to him, 'What are these wounds between your arms?' Then he will say, 'Those with which I was wounded in the house of my friends.'" (family)
Zechariah 13:6
Long after the wound heals, the scars remain.
JJB

Chapter 10
The Results of Abuse

The results of abuse, whether physical, emotional or sexual, are devastating. Though each individual will cope with trauma differently, all victims are traumatized to an extent beyond the plan and purpose of our Creator. In this section, the symptoms common to children of abuse will be reviewed with the hope that greater awareness of the effects will be helpful in your counseling ministry. This information can be used both diagnostically, and as a teaching component of your counseling.

The Symptoms

Firstly, children can experience many difficulties due to childhood abuse. Typically, what a counselor or parent should be aware of is a dramatic change in behavior or demeanor, or a continual pattern of these symptoms over time. All children may have some of these symptoms during times of "normal stress". The symptoms of child abuse include withdrawal from normal social encounters, to include friends and family. Fears can be manifested, to include nightmares, fear of undressing or of being left alone or with a certain person (uncle, babysitter, etc.). Severe expressions of anger, violent play or self-punishing behavior may occur. Finally, some children will try to compensate for their low self-esteem with a pseudo-adult maturity. This is a mask for the deep pains that the child is experiencing.

Females will experience many of the following symptoms in childhood, but may have repressed the events to survive. In late adolescence and adulthood, the symptoms which may indicate abuse include: memory blocks of periods of their childhood, secrecy about areas of their life and family, nightmares or insomnia over several months or even years, seductive behavior and promiscuity, and severe anxiety (panic attacks), depression and even eating disorders are common. Finally, co-dependent relationships often develop, and adult physical/sexual abuse may be the result. Of course, every person is unique, and can display additional symptoms. These are the most commonly seen in the counseling office.

Though less talked about, men do experience abuse. The effects are quite disturbing. They include depression, anxiety and frequent self-hatred to the point of suicidal ideation. Most often the symptoms are somatisized into stomach disorders. The major betrayal that has occurred, especially if the abuse has been of a homosexual nature, scars the identity, creating confusion and difficulty in developing intimacy.

The effects of sexual abuse go beyond simple symptom development. As pointed out in Dr. Allender's book, the *Wounded Heart* (Allender 1990), the problems created affect the core of the individual's personality. He listed four primary areas of pervasive repercussions caused by sexual abuse, which can be, with certain modification, generalized to all abuse.

Powerlessness

Abuse deprives a person of the sense of personal power. When a person is abused, especially as a child, the sense of freedom to choose, to self motivate, or to give self-direction is stripped away. Abuse generally occurs within the family setting, which should be a place of "safety." The individual learns that his/her environment is unsafe, and must learn to adapt to the environment to survive. All of the child's or spouse's energy,

energy needed for growth in the life cycle, is taken for personal survival. Therefore, what is learned is that "I have no power" or "I must conform to the authority over me." A further contributor to this sense of powerlessness comes from the normal child's' self-perception. Children believe that good things happen to good people, bad things happen to bad people. Thus, if the very worst possible thing that could have happened to me has indeed occurred, I must be a most horrible child. Thus, I must have deserved what has occurred, and deserve punishment. This perception, very black and white in nature, must be gently confronted and clarified for healing to occur.

The powerlessness that develops causes severe self-doubt (I can't do anything, I am worthless), despair of the circumstances of life (I can't change, this is just the way my life is), and deadness, or the inability to feel anything, neither pleasure nor pain. This leads to an overwhelming sense of loss of self, the ability to make decisions or have adequate adult judgment, or to care and protect oneself from present and future harm. Also, this powerlessness is the reason that men and women who have been abused do not "see" the abuse of their own children. The numbing of the self makes awareness of danger for the self or others most difficult. The child will introject (turn inside) the blame for the abuse on themselves.

Betrayal

The first stage of our development as presented by Erickson is Trust vs. Mistrust. Trust is the foundation upon which all growth in relationships is built. When abuse occurs in the family, regardless of the age in which it occurs, the ability to trust is violated. This sense of betrayal in a relationship is most devastating. The adult has projected their needs onto the child, violating the sacred trust. The violation of trust opens the door to feelings of shame and guilt, which are most often discussed by abuse victims. Further, due to the dynamics of family life and relationships in general, the one betrayed often falsely believes that he/she could/should have done something to keep the victimization from occurring. Perhaps if the one betrayed had been less needy or vulnerable, the abuse would not have happened. This powerful internalized and often ritualized lie is one of the major barriers to the healing process. Much of the therapy process will focus on and must address this internalized lie.

The betrayal can create in the victim such problems as hyper-vigilance (perfectionism and extreme self - consciousness), paranoia (better thought of as suspiciousness), which makes the ability to have a satisfactory intimate relationship nearly impossible. The strongest defense used by most victims is that of denial, which includes a distortion of the truth that must be faced, if the victim will ever be truly free.

Ambivalence

Dr. Allender defined ambivalence as "feeling two contradictory emotions at the same moment" (Allender. 1990). A joke that illustrates ambivalence is the person watching his mother-in-law drive his new Lexus (slight update) over a cliff. The point is, when two strong emotions, such as love/hate, honor/betrayal, trust/fear are combined, confusion and misunderstanding can develop. The distorted feelings are created when a double message is experienced (I love you, so let me touch you/I want our marriage to work, so shut up and do as I tell you), which has no solution. The most difficult of all is the mixture of pleasure and pain that all sexual abuse victims experience. God made our bodies, regardless of age, to respond to stimulation. When the body feels pleasure, but the mind knows the wrongfulness of the stimulation, a tremendous twisting of truth to tolerate the experience occurs. Untwisting the lies, resolving the ambivalence, can only be done by the power of the Holy Spirit and wise, professional counsel.

Relational Style

All victimization, especially when prolonged over time, will inevitably create a pattern of relating which will perpetuate the victimization. This can be most frustrating, as a therapist, as you watch your client enter into the same problems over and over again. It is important to remember that the client does not want the patterns that have developed. They want more than you to be well, productive and happy in their life. However, since the only models provided for them as children or in a marital relationship have been abusive, the pattern of victim or victimizer becomes fixated, dysfunctional communication and often destructive behavior will be the ultimate result.

The relational style is primarily the daily mask that the client wears to protect him/herself from the world. Often a "social trance" occurs allowing for the continuation of abuse generationally. This self-protective style of relating to people keeps one from growing. One of the key ingredients in counseling is vulnerability, or the modeling of honesty in relationships. Though not trusted, sometimes for weeks and months, the counselor must work through this resistance (it's not personal!) to bring lasting relief and restoration for the counselee. The Lord has called us all to be conformed to the image of Christ. This can only occur as we "renew our mind" (process, not event), through the Word of God and effective healing prayer. This will be discussed in detail in the sections on treatment.

For Class Discussion

1. Discuss the various symptoms of abuse. Can you think of more than those listed in this section?

2. Discuss the concept of generational abuse.

3. Discuss the Relational Style of the victim. Can you think of someone with this relational style that might indicate abuse?

"How poor are they that have not patience. What wound did ever heal but by degrees"

William Shakespeare, Othello, II iii, 379

"Do not imagine that you in the king's palace can escape any more than all the Jews. For if you remain silent at this time, relief and deliverance will arise for the Jews from another place and you and your father's house will perish. And who knows whether you have not attained royalty for such a time as this?"

Esther 4:13-14

One ship sails East, one ship sails West by the self same wind that blows;
It is not the wind but the set of the sails that determines which way we will go.
Anon.

Chapter 11
Crisis Management

When the initial reporting or discovery of the abuse occurs, the need for crisis counseling or management is evident. As a Pastor, lay leader or Christian counselor, you will want to be as supportive as possible in your treatment of the victim. Their initial reactions are usually masks to guard themselves from further violation. Again, it is important that you not take this defensiveness personally, but in the love of Christ accept the person where they are and skillfully assist in the management of the components of crisis.

In this chapter, the dynamics of crises are discussed, from a theoretical and biblical basis. For a more thorough development of crisis counseling from a biblical perspective, see the book by Dr. Stan DeKoven, *Crisis Counseling* (DeKoven. 2003*).*

The Crisis in Abuse

When a report is received or a referral is made where domestic violence or child abuse is alleged, the feeling of crisis will be most evident. Even in the situation where measures of safety have been taken (the child has been removed from the home, the husband/wife has moved out), the potential volatility of the situation remains. The hurts and anger expressed by the victim and victimizer alike will run hot, and will require swift and decisive response on behalf of the counselor, welfare worker, medical professional or pastor. Before looking at specific interventions, definitions are in order.

A crisis can be seen as a "turning point in anything; decisive or crucial time, stage, or event; a time of great danger or trouble, whose outcome decides whether possible bad consequences will follow." (Webster) The crisis of abuse of any kind is a situation, which temporarily changes the real world of the abused and abuser, and necessitates an often times radical emotional, physical and spiritual adjustment to life.

The crises of abuse will have detrimental effects on all parties involved. For example, the whole family will become victims in an incest situation. However, the ultimate impact on the family or members thereof will be determined by the meaning that is given to the event and the overall ability of the family to cope with the high level of stress created by the abuse. The power found in any crisis is related to two factors:

1) The closeness of the event.
2) Perception of the meaning of the event.

The case of the Smithton's

When the Smithton's were first referred to me the family was in a state of chaos. The father had been rightly removed from the home for having fondled his eldest daughter. This horribly inappropriate behavior had been going on with Amanda, his 12 year old daughter for the past 18 months, but had recently been exposed when Amanda confided in a girl friend who told the teacher who called the police. At the first counseling session, which included the whole family (not always a good idea), the father showed up by the mother's invitation, against court orders. I permitted him to stay in the session, but called the social worker while he was in the office to receive permission for his involvement. It was permitted with a strong and appropriate reprimand.

When we began the session, Amanda was very quiet as

were her younger brother and sister. Mrs. Smithton (Jill Ann) was also extremely reserved, allowing her husband (no doubt out of fear and intimidation) to have the floor. I permitted and encouraged Mr. Smithton's diatribe of venom and accusation to flow for a season. He blamed his wife's lack of affection, the daughter's promiscuous desires for a boy friend and the lack of pastoral care for his behavior. He admitted reluctantly his guilt for the molestation, but summed it all up with a declaration that he should be allowed to come home since the whole affair was now "forgiven and under the blood!" It was at that point that Mrs. Smithton, Amanda and I joined forces in dealing with the scoundrel in as vociferous a manner as possible…the outrage and arrogance of the man was only too typical. I spoke first, declaring the inappropriateness and insensitivity of his outrageous statement and projection of blame. I further spoke to the theological inaccuracy of his supposition, yes the sin might be forgiven but the consequences were not fully played out and healing was still very much in need. Next, Jill Ann spoke from a reservoir of rage that must have been repressed for many years as she shouted at him that he would never return to her home after what he had done to her and her daughter. Finally, Amanda burst into tears, apologizing to everyone for having caused such a problem. She knew it was all her fault. She wanted her mom and dad to just get along, and stated her willingness to leave the home so everything would be all right. And that was just the beginning. After settling everyone down from the highly tense encounter, I was able to begin to intervene in the situation. However, the level of tension and misunderstandings boarding on delusion are not untypical in an abusive family circumstance as described here.

Phases of a Crisis

H. Norman Wright in his excellent book *Crisis Counseling: Helping People in Crisis and Stress* outlines four primary phases of crisis.

They are:

1) Impact
2) Withdrawal Confusion
3) Adjustment
4) Reconstruction/Reconciliation

An understanding of these four phases can assist the counselor in minimizing the damage of the crisis and lead the family or individual in the direction of successful solution.

I. Impact

Our initial response to a domestic violence crisis is determined by the impact that the abuse has upon the client, the meaning that is given the event and the duration or levels of the abuse itself. The impact can only be measured by the response that the individual or family has toward the crisis situation. For some people, the smallest situations can create great anxiety, sadness or depression. Many others, because of a high tolerance for pain or a fairly peace-oriented spirit, are able to flow through many crises without great difficulty. How we respond depends upon many factors including:

1) The genetic predisposition toward stress and its' management
2) The spiritual vitality of the individual(s) or family
3) The understanding of the Word of God and its' application
4) The support systems such as family and friendships both within and outside the body of Christ
5) The history in regards to the management of crisis situations in the family and the amount and type of abuse presented.

Needless to say, the impact of a crisis cannot fully be

understood until the crisis occurs. In the case of the Smithton's, each member of the family responded differently to the crisis. Dad responded with initial remorse then rage, mom with depression and withdrawal, Amanda with fear and sadness, and the other siblings with a bit of bewilderment and loss of security. Obviously, the whole family was affected by dad's impulsive acting out behavior, made worse by his narcissistic desire to return to the family as though nothing had happened.

II. Withdrawal/Confusion

When a crisis occurs, a scapegoat or cause for the abuse is generally looked for. A desire to understand why is natural, and general confusion is the norm. I remember as a child when my father came home from work and declared that he had lost his job (a rather frequent occurrence in our family). I just could not understand how my father, my hero could always run afoul of his boss. I did not fully understand that my dad often acted out his insecurity by threatening and in more than one occasion hitting a boss, a sure way to ruin a budding career.

To my father's credit, he did not fully blame his bosses for his temper, but often did in his younger days project blame on my mom. This led to many a terrible shouting match, and great disturbance for my sister, brother and myself.

When the crisis of the week would occur in our home, I would find myself lost in my own thoughts, and would hole up in my sister's bedroom. The three of us (my brother, sister and me) would try and pretend to not hear the shouting and threats, but could not help but internalize the terror of the time. Essentially, I felt a sense of confusion and loss. This is not unusual in times of crisis. When someone is abused or becomes aware of abusive patterns there can be a time of withdrawal or confusion that can be virtually immobilizing. Great care, support and careful counsel can assist the abused in working through the initial phases of crisis.

III. Adjustment

The crisis in the Smithton family required significant adjustment to lifestyle and expectations. With the father being removed from the home, the economic viability of the family became suspect. Basic securities were threatened, and compromised the treatment process. The level of denial of the father made the adjustment process even more difficult. He was initially unwilling to assist economically or in any other way, since in his mind he was coming home any day (this is one reason why we often need the intervention of the court as an ally for us). Amanda, the primary victim in the abuse had to adjust to a new role in the family as mother support with the younger children, as mom had to obtain work for the first time in her life. This unfair reality made her decision to tell, seem less the right thing to do.

All people will adjust to a crisis in their own elegant style. We must allow time for people to make adjustment; although we must watch for signs of their staying in a withdrawn and confused state beyond what is psychologically and spiritually healthy. The relative ability to make good adjustment will be dependent on many factors, the chief being the history of the family's dealings with past crises and the extent of the abuse over time.

IV. Reconstruction/Reconciliation

The long-term goal of counseling is problem resolution. The problem with the problem of abuse is its' diabolical nature. It is not easy to fix the betrayal of one family member abusing another, though that is the hope. Reconstruction or reconciliation of the family after domestic violence will often take months and even years. However, all things are possible with Christ, when the members of the family are willing to do the hard work of facing the truth and allowing the healing of Christ and his church to occur.

Solutions to a Crisis Situation

The role of the counselor in the crisis situation is to bring and maintain control. Each counselor must evaluate his or her ability to tolerate conflict and manage it in a counseling setting. I for one can even escalate or allow the escalation of intense feelings in a family with relative aplomb. Perhaps this is due to my early life experience with my family of origin. This will not be true for every counselor, and one should error on the side of safety first. However, whatever the crisis, there is always a solution. The solutions are rarely easy and often require creative thought and planning. It is important to recognize that there are solutions to any crisis.

In order to solve a crisis, we must be willing to face the problem. Galatians 6:1 presents a biblical basis for the need to face the truth, and to work diligently towards restoration. It is the responsibility of the mature to assist the wounded (even if self-inflicted) to overcome sin and return to productive living. First, we must help the one in crisis to face the truth of their crisis with courage and care.

Secondly, in dealing with a crisis, our goal is to assist the family or individual to untangle their projection system. That is, to help them to look at things in a more appropriate way. The more religious a person is the more difficult the task can be, as can be seen in the case of Mr. Smithton.

Third, we assist the abused and abuser alike in expressing their feelings in an appropriate manner, to speak the truth in love. The victims especially need the opportunity to share their story with acceptance and empathy, and tell is as often as necessary.

A model for crisis counseling that is simple and effective is the A.B.C.D. model of crisis intervention. This can be used most effectively in the planning of crisis intervention and in the actual working through of a crisis.

ACHIEVE a relationship. To achieve a relationship it is important to listen, fully, to the individual's problem without judgment, and with great empathy. The listening process demonstrates that we care and are willing to assist the individual in the resolution of the conflict. Presenting trite clichés or pretending to be interested when we really are not can cause severe damage to the client at a time of heightened vulnerability. The goal is to first achieve a relationship with the individual who is having the crisis through active listening, empathy, warmth and respect.

BOIL down the problem. Most people in a crisis believe there circumstances are astronomical and overwhelming. They often express feelings of hopelessness, and lack a vision or the overall resolve to survive or manage the conflict. Part of assisting them is to break down the components of the problem into smaller bites. Most any problem, when viewed through the eyes of the one in crisis can seem insurmountable. Thus, the counselor or pastor must assist the client by boiling down the problem into more manageable components. Handling the newly revealed knowledge of a husband's infidelity and the possible loss of hearth and home is too much for many a victim, but handling how to get through tomorrow is possible for most.

CHALLENGE the individual to take constructive action. This requires looking at things one piece at a time, assisting the person or family to deal with, "What can I do now? What can I do tomorrow? What can I do to resolve the overall problem?" It is vital that the individual in the crisis, with your assistance, develops a positive or constructive action to meet the present need. Always remember it is safety first in all situations. Avoid where you can reasonably do so the potential mistake of advice giving, rather than exploring alternatives that are then chosen by the counselee. If you just give them advice, telling them what to do, you will find yourself frustrated often. The frustration comes because you are trying to solve the problem for them rather than allowing them the dignity of coming up with solutions for themselves. We need to allow them to solve the problem the best that they can, trusting that, with God's help, they will be able to do so.

DEVELOP an ongoing plan of action. A one-shot counseling session is rarely efficacious in a crisis. There must be an ongoing relationship and plan of action developed with the client. This plan should be written down, thus creating commitment and accountability. Develop goals that will make a difference. The long-term goal of insight or understanding as to how they became vulnerable to this crisis may come later. Subsequent to this level of insight would be to learn how to cope more effectively or even avoid similar crisis in the future. This takes a commitment on behalf of the counselor as well, a commitment we must be prepared to make if we are to be truly therapeutic and Christ like.

For Class Discussion

1. What is a crisis? What is not a crisis?

2. Discuss the phases of a crisis.

3. Discuss the A.B.C.D. model of crisis intervention.

4. If you were faced with the Smithton family, what might your approach be? What goals would you set for them, both short and long-term?

"They heal the brokenness of the daughter of My people superficially, saying 'Peace, peace' But there is no peace. Were they ashamed because of the abomination they had done? They certainly were not ashamed, and they did not know how to blush."

Jeremiah 8:11-12

"Surely our griefs He Himself bore, And our sorrows He carried; Yet we ourselves esteemed Him stricken, Smitten of God, and afflicted. But he was pierced through for our transgressions, He was crushed for our iniquities; The chastening for our well-being fell upon Him, And by his scourging we are healed."

Isaiah 53:4-5

A wise physician is John the Baptist, who recognizes that his only mission is to prepare the way for a greater than himself.
Arthur S. Hardy
He who has health has hope, and he who has hope has everything.
Arabian Proverb

Chapter 12
Treatment Process

There are always strategies that can be recommended; most have proven effective in certain situations. However, no one treatment strategy will work with all clients. Therefore, the more we know and the more comfortable we become with the human tragedy, the better able we will function as counselors in the therapeutic process.

Most counseling delete will follow a process that can be broken down into different phases. There is no clear demarcation in terms of when a client is done with one phase and thus beginning another. Each client will be different, and we must be flexible in our counseling process and goals.

Initial Phase

It has been said (by me I think) that counseling begins with the phone call (or first contact). The person making the call is usually the one with the greatest emotional distress.

Problems do not occur in isolation from family dynamics. Each individual in the family will have a part to play, and in many cases even multigenerational dynamics can be a part (see I Want To Be Like You, Dad, by DeKoven). The key is to recognize that the family is generally the client, not just the individual, and the communication process is what must be examined and often modified to bring about change.

When first meeting a client, whether individual, couple, or family, it is recommended that the SOAP method of information gathering be adopted. The SOAP stands for a simple acronym meaning Self, Other, Assessment and Plan. Each part is important and discussed in light of the following case study.

The Hernandez Family

Mr. Hernandez (Jorge or George) was a third generation Hispanic businessman with a highly successful career. He was married to Maria, a first generation Hispanic woman from Guatemala. They had been married for nearly 12 years with three children and one on the way. Mr. Hernandez was referred to counseling after having been arrested for assault and battery on his wife, and possible physical assault on their 12 year old son. The son had apparently stepped into the middle of a fight between his father and mother, essentially stating that he could not take his dad beating up his mom anymore. Maria had been hospitalized (broken jaw and multiple lacerations of her head and face) by the latest abuse at the hands of George, had filed for divorce, though George was hopeful that reconciliation might be possible. He had spent 90 days in prison for his assault, was now on probation, and during his time in prison had had a conversion to Christianity. His hope for counseling was to rebuild his family life, and start again now that he was "born again".

Self

When you initially encounter a client, you need to be aware of your own feelings towards the client, your perceptions, and your attitudes. When first interviewing Mr. Hernandez I was struck with his initial denial and arrogance. I suspected some of the arrogance as it is common for Hispanic males (other nationalities as well) to be "machismo" or macho in perspective, but his machismo was beyond the norm in light of the obvious offense against his bride and family. How do we feel as the client shares their story with us is an indicator of how others may respond, and a good diagnostic indicator. I was outraged at his presentation, yet felt some sense of his charm in how he presented himself. The questions to ask oneself during and after an interview include was I angry, sad, hurt, scared, confused, manipulated, etc. by the client? Whatever the feelings, they are to be noted in the Counselors log or on notebook paper. How we initially experience the client is often an indicator of how others respond to the family or person. Though the observations of our self and the feelings we experience may be helpful and relatively accurate, we must be careful not to make judgments based upon this information alone. We still need much more than feelings before deciding on a course of action in treatment.

Other

Observation of the client interaction, from where they sit to their conversation is an essential aspect of talk therapy. My observation of Mr. Hernandez was essential in the treatment process. He started his defense of himself with statements of innocence, but quickly reverted to remorseful statements and a posture of submission when even lightly confronted about his abusive behavior.

All counselors must be acute observers of human behavior. We must have a working knowledge of why humans do what they do as we observe the clients' behavior. Again, there are questions we are to ask ourselves as we work with the client, including why would they act in such a way? What motivates them to make certain life decisions? Where did they learn their dysfunctional or functional patterns of living? What additional information do I need that has not been revealed thus far, and how should I obtain it?

These and other pertinent questions must be made once the client has told their story, and revealed their feelings. Further, we must ascertain how their belief systems have allowed for the present situation to occur, bringing them to their present life circumstance. Of course, it is important to not assume too much, but only believe what we are certain of. All hypotheses must be tested.

Assessment

After the initial session or two, after they have told their story (all members of a family must have the opportunity to speak their mind and heart. Domination of the session by a client or yourself is not permitted) we must develop a preliminary assessment of the client. This can include areas that need further exploration, through tests or questionnaires. In the beginning of your counseling ministry, it is best to err on the side of too much information rather than not enough. The assessment should include the history of the client, when the symptoms began, how the family or individual has coped thus far, what has worked and what has not, and your impressions of the underlying dynamics of the case. In most cases, a DSM-IV diagnosis is not necessary, but it is good to be familiar with the classification system, and practice good diagnostic methodology.

In the case of Mr. Hernandez, the diagnosis was somewhat simple. He was an angry and defensive man with limited sense of responsibility in terms of his behavior, and a limited capacity to gain insight from the therapeutic process. Much of his defensiveness was cultural in nature. However, he was interested in gaining entrance to his family, and thus was willing to consider the therapeutic interventions suggested by the counselor.

Once the counselor has developed the initial thoughts regarding the case, it is most helpful to share the case with a learned colleague, while insuring confidentiality of the client. A supervisor or colleague can assist in seeing any insights that may have been missed in the initial assessment. No counselor is infallible, and outside input can cover a multiple of miss-diagnosed clients. Finally, in all assessments, it is important to find something good, some component of the personality of the client that is commendable or redeemable. It is always helpful to like the client. Mr. Hernandez actually had an engaging and warm personality, despite his Cro-Magnon man approach to life. This assisted me in the confrontation of his behavior and theology. The bible clearly states that we are to love our neighbors, and especially those the Lord has allowed us to be in relationship with in the counseling office.

Plan

The development of a treatment plan is as important as the development of a business plan. Without it, unless you are a highly seasoned veteran, you will likely spend much time wandering in the "counseling wilderness." The treatment plan should contain all of what has been previously obtained, test information that may have been gathered, and an actual idea of the direction to take in the treatment process. The counselor and the client need specific goals to accomplish, such as reduction of anger by 50% (one of the goals of Mr. Hernandez, as demonstrated by no verbal or physical outbursts), or more intimacy, as demonstrated by dating and communication exercises, etc. The goals should be measurable where possible and should be developed with the assistance of the client(s), and in keeping with our expertise, client time frame, and financial means. Many clients do not desire a total life transformation. Remember that we did not cause the brokenness in the clients' life, and we cannot fix them. Only the grace and mercy of the Lord Jesus Christ and the power of his word applied to their lives can produce real and life long change.

For Class Discussion

1. Summarize the Hernandez case in your own words, and give some additional insight as to how you might have approached counseling him.

"So the helpless has hope, And unrighteousness must shut its mouth."

Job 5:16

"Namely, that God was in Christ reconciling the world to Himself, not counting their trespasses against them, and He has committed to us the word of reconciliation."
2 Corinthians 5:19

Chapter 13
Major Modes of Marital Counseling

Before doing marital therapy, especially with domestic violence cases, it is important to understand a variety of marital therapy modalities. Several modalities are presented here by way of review.

Psychodynamic Marital Therapy

Psychodynamic Marital Therapy's basic assumption is the reciprocal relationship between conflict among family members and conflict within the mind of any one member. Its origin is rooted in the psychoanalytic tradition. The therapeutic focus is on the interpersonal and intra-psychic conflict, which feed upon one another in a circular fashion. The therapist is more interested in the family history than most family therapists. This type of therapy is often indicated for serious, long-standing emotional problems that have resisted other therapy and very often will involve several generations of family members.

Family myths and secrets are brought into the open during treatment. Actual facts and events known to some family members and not to others may emerge. Some events or conditions not allowed to be discussed are talked about, such as alcoholism. Skeletons that embarrass the family, such as imprisonment, institutionalization in a mental hospital, an illegitimate pregnancy, or a defection from the armed forces, are talked about as well. Ghosts in the family, whether living or dead, are an unfinished topic in the family. It could be an unmourned death or a living person who may be brought into the therapeutic process.

Social Learning -- Cognitive Marital Therapy

The Social Learning - Cognitive Marital Therapy (SLC) is characterized by a dual emphasis on the social environment and cognitive-perceptual processes as the determining factors of behavior. The approach is based on the assumption that behavior change is not only important, but offers a basis for producing cognitive and affective changes.

Another premise of this therapy is that skills are required in order to maintain a satisfactory intimate relationship over a long period of time. Love and attraction are not enough to sustain a relationship. A variety of skills are needed, including the ability to deal constructively with conflict, provide support and understanding to one another, and to perform affectionately. The therapist must identify the areas of deficiency and develop a plan for change.

Reinforcement erosion is another major treatment focus. There is a natural tendency for spouses in a long-term relationship to gradually lose their ability to gratify one another. Therapists help the couple to track relationship quality on a day-to-day basis and devote the time and attention to it required to maintain a high level of marital satisfaction.

Structural-Strategic Marital Therapy

Structural Marital Therapy is directed toward changing the organization of the family. When the structure is changed, the relative (and often entrenched) positions of the members are also changed. As a result, each of the individuals experiences and perceptions of self and other change. Therapy is based on the fact that the individual is not an isolate, but an acting and reacting member of a social group.

Salvador Minuchin is the founder of structural marital

therapy. He was working with poor families struggling day-to-day for survival. His approach was oriented towards solving problems that were immediate and real. His focus is on the relationships that connect one part of the whole to another. It is a therapy of action. The focus is to modify the present, not to explore and interpret the past.

Strategic Marital Therapy's major assumptions are in ongoing interactive sessions within the family, the practitioner is the primary source of change rather than the client, and problem formation and resolution rather than helping the client grow. The basic theoretical view of this approach is that clients come for help because they do not handle everyday problems of living. The therapist's skillful use of directives is an art. The therapist must motivate the individual, couple or family to follow his direction. Rapport and trust must be established. The therapist gives precise and clear direction, and if the first strategy does not work, a second directive is given. A distinguishing quality of strategic therapy is the use of positive connotation or reframing. The behaviors of the client are accepted without labeling them as resistant. Minuchin also discovered the multi-generational aspect of psychopathology in the family, addressing it in the hear and now.[4]

Bowen Family Systems Family Therapy

In Bowen Family Therapy, the importance of theory to guide a therapist is emphasized rather than an intuitive, spontaneous, emotional, or non-theoretical approach. Murray Bowen, the founder, contends that emotional disturbances develop from relationships with others and are maintained by those relationships. There are eight interlocking theoretical concepts that are forces for shaping family functioning. They are differentiation of self, triangles, nuclear family emotional system, family

---

[4] see I Want To Be Like You, Dad, by Dr. DeKoven for more on Generational Patterns

projection process, emotional cut off, multi - generational transmission process, sibling position, and societal regression.

Bowen suggests that the therapist take the position of the significant other to help modify the relationships within the family. He advises the therapist to remain uninvested in the family conflict to avoid triangulation. His goals are for each family member to maximize their self-differentiation within the nuclear family and from the family of origin.

Marital Enrichment and Prevention

An alternative approach to the marital distress models is intervention through preventative psychoeducative programs. Unlike treatment or enrichment, prevention occurs before any symptoms of relational distress develop. It is future oriented and only indirectly addresses the current difficulties premarital couples may be experiencing. Relationship enhancement is included as a preventative function to couples who are already experiencing high levels of satisfaction, in the hope of preventing future problems.

Prevention, ideally, starts with premarital counseling. One such program is the Premarital Relationship Enhancement Program (PREP), a cognitive-behaviorally oriented intervention. The program helps couples develop competency in communication and problem-solving skills to increase the probability that they will achieve successful marriages. The couples solve low-conflict relationship problems to increase their confidence in their ability to solve more serious problems in the future.

The PREP program also covers sensual-sexual enhancement, which increases the couples' knowledge of human sexual functioning and decreases misconceptions without intruding on their moral beliefs. It covers relationship beliefs and expectations about children, careers, and role responsibilities. Communication proficiency is evaluated, obtaining both subjective and objective assessments of problem-solving interactional skills. Relationship satisfaction and areas of agreement-disagreement are evaluated using the Premarital Adjustment Test to evaluate the overall level of relationship satisfaction and areas in which the couples perceive themselves as agreeing and disagreeing such as finances and displays of affection. Many other programs such as PREP are readily available on the market for the trained counselors usage.

Assessing Distressed Marriages

Assessment is the process of describing the interaction between client and the arresting obstacle of their surroundings. Direct observation rather than inferences from surface cues make it reliable. Assessment describes productive and unproductive elements of the client's behavior and offers immediate relevance to therapeutic planning. Assessment surpasses diagnosis in reliability and validity and serves as a foundation for the collection and analysis of data. Assessment is an ongoing process that covers the period of time before the first contact and ends long after the last treatment session.

The assessment must broaden the partners' perspectives to include awareness of their own roles. The data collected must be strength oriented and positive. A new respect for the couples' strengths can replace their dirty laundry lists about each other and a new hope will emerge knowing there are resources available for change.

Boundary conditions affect marital interaction and satisfaction. They can predispose them to positive joyful interactions or to negative and highly stressful experiences. They do not determine the success of the marriage, but they do influence the challenges and the effort that must by put forth for success. Some controllable conditions would include: cultural attitudes, life stresses, aging and illnesses. Couples can also control the way they see and handle these events, for instance, by thinking of obstacles as opportunities. It is possible to control the way in which they react to these events.

Communication Techniques

Communication is basic to the survival of all organisms. Skill is needed to send information and to receive and interpret the data. One of the primary goals for marital therapy are to build the couples' communication skills, to make their desires known, to understand the other's requests, and to gain a common understanding. Especially with highly dysfunctional families, and most definitely with domestic violence cases, communication enhancement and adjustment are vital. A five-step program to help achieve these goals is:

1. **The Ability to Listen**. Good listeners are able to separate their emotions from the other's words. Effective listening requires considerable effort. Good listeners are fully committed to listening, are physically and mentally ready to listen, wait for the other to complete the message before expressing their own ideas, and use analytic skills to supplement listening and not replace it. These skills give the listener the ability to help the speaker feel accepted and understood.
2. **Constructive Request-Making**. Couples have a tendency to be quite indirect with their requests from spouses. Their requests are not openly expressed. They are disguised in sweet suggestions or questions and accusations with much manipulation. Appropriate phrasing of their requests must be taught, as well as when to express their requests. In most families, the members have learned to say please, but they often have not learned how to read the cues of the other's readiness to hear, let alone grant requests.
3. **Selective, Specific and Timely Feedback**. The way in which the couple express their reaction to one another's behavior helps to improve the quality of their communication. It reduces uncertainty. Feedback is necessary in order to adequately perform any kind of social

or physical task. Direct and honest feedback in families in general is very rare, nearly non-existent in the violent family system. Positive feedback rather than negative feedback brings change. It is possible to stimulate better outcomes, positive risk-taking, and higher performance result, with positive feedback.

4. **Clarification.** This is simply to clarify the message that has been received. Pseudo communication is an illusion of understanding in which both spouses think they have shared an understanding of a given situation but each has grossly misunderstood the other. Training in how to clarify speech is taught in most communication programs. Validation or confirming/clarifying are terms often used in teaching these techniques. The couples practice a two-phase clarification process, instigating them to ask for meaning and then to restate the message received. The listener should probe the speaker for additional data until he/she can accurately paraphrase the speaker's message. This process is quite tedious for the participants, as spontaneous emission of thought is the norm. Yet, with practice and positive reinforcement, which comes through encouragement by the counselor, these skills can be learned.

5. **Self-expression**. Self-expressive statements help partners orient themselves to each other and to help each person make sense of his or her own experience by putting that experience into words. Clients in communication programs are taught the use of self-statement, including:

   a. The "I rule (I feel, I think, versus you statements, which causes defensiveness),"
   b. The "statement rule, (make clear and precise statements directive rather than inquisitive)"
   c. The "say-ask rule (say what you are thinking and then ask your partner if they understood)"

d. The "how rule (such as how do you see this rather than the more defensive why did you do this or that statement)",
e. The "two-questions rule (rather than overwhelming with a dozen shot-gun questions"
f. The "now rule (versus the you did something 7 years ago and I am going to beat you over the head and shoulders today with it statement)," and
g. The "simplicity speaks-the-truth rule (or again, be direct rather than convoluted in dialogue, or better yet monologue)."

Each of these rules, judiciously followed can assist the most dysfunctional couple or family learn to communicate effectively. The counselor is tasked to model these forms of communication, and teach the techniques with ample opportunity for practice for the clients.

Reciprocity Techniques

Reciprocal determinism is the belief that all behavior is always reciprocally (repaid) interactive with the social, physical, and personal environments in which it occurs (or you reap what you sow). The individual is actively creating his or her own environment or the environment has been constructed in their head and is the environment they respond to.

Reciprocity between couples is common. It is the "voluntary actions of individuals who are motivated by the returns that they expect, and typically do bring from others" (Blau, 1964). It is not necessarily a calculated and self-serving motive. Couples today express a high degree of commitment to the ideal of reciprocal, equalitarian marriage, but it does not imply symmetry nor equality, but equity. The expectations of one's spouse to immediately reciprocate can often lead to frustration and anger.

While strangers may reciprocate immediately, spouses don't and the expectation that they will may contribute to shattered illusions. While reciprocity may be the norm that maintains all stable reactions, a mature expectation recognizes that the debts are more likely to be paid next month or next year as opposed to tomorrow. Reciprocity among mature, stable relationships are viewed as a norm. Spouses either feel well compensated for their investments into the relationship when they expect and receive a just return, or feel ill-used when they believe they have been and will continually give substantially more than they are getting. Stability of the relationship is increased when spouse's investment increases in light of their potential returns and costs. Instability stems from everything in the relationship being evaluated by both parties in terms of potential rewards. This is the common stance taken by families involved in domestic violence, further complicating the counseling process.

Treatment of Spousal Abuse With Conjoint Marital Therapy

As a part of the treatment of spousal abuse utilizing techniques of crisis intervention, transitional counseling is frequently needed. This can include obtaining emergency leave, planned exit from the home, financial support and support for children, etc. Further, a clear assessment of the level and types of abuse must be determined, and appropriate planned action implemented.

Where Post-traumatic Stress Disorder is found, individual therapy is needed. Couple therapy, family treatment and skill training groups are recommended.

A recent article in *Family Therapy Today* stated that, "Domestic violence has finally been recognized as an epidemic, and substantial media attention has recently been devoted to this crime. It is now estimated, when the results of various incidence studies of family violence are reviewed, that spouse abuse (physical, sexual, verbal, or emotional) occurs at least once in 20-30% of all families. In the majority of cases, it is the woman who is battered, yet in about 10% of the cases, it is the man who is battered. In many cases there is mutual violence; but even in these situations it is the woman who usually gets hurt (Straus & Gelles, 1986). Every 18 seconds in the United States, a woman is beaten by her partner. Because spouse abuse is so prevalent, it is very important for marriage and family therapists to be fully cognizant of this problem and to become familiar with treatment techniques.

A Conjoint Approach

There are different techniques proposed to reduce wife abuse, including individual and group treatment, usage of battered womens' shelters, or anger management programs for batterers. Probably the most controversial approach used today is conjoint therapy. It is controversial because the counseling service works with the man and the woman conjointly (Geller & Wasserstrom, 1984, Harris, 1986). The intervention technique is basically psychoeducational and eclectic.

This positive treatment choice is indicated as an option for those couples who want to end the violence and intimidation, remain in an improved relationship, and participate in counseling together. The fear of losing the relationship is a powerful motivator for both partners.

Abusers and victims indicated that both batterers and battered women had many similar characteristics. The results of extensive psychological, marital, and social evaluations indicated that both the men and the women exhibited anger, hostility, impulsivity, low self-esteem, and lack of assertiveness, stress, marital dissatisfaction, poor communication skills, and abuse of alcohol. These problem areas need to be addressed even if they are the result of the partners living in an abusive situation.

Conjoint therapy has the advantage of not only working with the couple to reduce the violence but also to improve their relationship. This approach focuses on the dysfunctional relationship and helps both people change their individual ways of interacting as well as the relationship itself. The long-term goals are to reduce the batterer's violence and intimidation, empower the woman, and change the structure of the relationship. This is essential if one has hope of breaking the cycle of violence, since research indicates that the greatest risk factor for spouse abuse is being abused or witnessing abuse in the family of origin (Caesar, 1988, Hotaling & Sugarman, 1986).

A disadvantage of this conjoint approach is that both partners need to be willing to commit themselves to therapy. Further, there is the potential danger of additional violence if the couple remains together, so the therapist must be aware of this potential and focus on a cessation of violence commitment during the initial sessions. Of course, the couple does not have to be living together to make use of a conjoint approach.

Specific Techniques

In the initial stages, the couples sign a non-violence contract, again to ensure commitment and safety. This can be quite effective, especially since they often enter therapy during a "honeymoon" period following an abusive incident. The counselor must make it clear from the beginning, reinforced regularly, that violence is not acceptable under any condition. Abuse is a choice made by the individual, and he/she is responsible for his/her own behavior. The ideas of responsibility and choice as well as safety precautions for the woman, emergency plans and telephone numbers and maintenance of the non-violent contract are regularly and emphatically reinforced.

The contract developed must include at a minimum the following (Geller. 1992):

1. Recognize the signals -- when the anger might escalate, sweaty palms, stomach knotting, increased heartbeat,

light-headedness, dizziness and body tension. When the batterer receives and becomes aware of these cues or anger, the contract must be employed. It is important to remember that "Batterers often feel victimized themselves. One author has noted that violence occurs when the batterer believes his partner is attacking his sense of self" (Geller. 1992. p.109).
2. Examine the various options -- what can the batterer do to avoid acting out? Such things as take a walk, jog, go to another room, etc. The options should be presented by the counselor but must be chosen by the batterer.
3. Determine to take time-out -- It is vitally important that the batterer ruthlessly determine to take time out (for 15 minutes or more, until calm and rational) before resuming dialog.
4. Directives must be given regarding the number of times that discussion is attempted to resolve conflict. No more than three attempts can be made until termination of attempts, or until the next day.
5. Bonding is to occur and ways found to strengthen and improve intimacy, communication and trust. Again, as counselors we are to make suggestions, but it is up to the wife (victim) to choose which methods are safe and acceptable.
6. Review of the contract -- is made weekly so that corrections can be made as required.
7. Repeat the process until there is "fruit of repentance" or a cessation of the acting out for a significant period of time (at least 90 days).

For most couples the initial sessions will focus on accusations and fault-finding for various behaviors. We emphasize a "no blame" approach similar to systems theory since we do not seek to punish either person. A "blame approach," if permitted to continue, would even further lower the self-esteem of the partners and tends to hinder the development of rapport with the therapist. It does not allow the therapist to act as a change agent in assisting the partners alter current and future behavior and attitudes. Explain that our job is not to judge and blame but rather to help them change so that they no longer use violence and intimidation and the victim no longer feels afraid of being hit. This no-blame approach seems to create a more positive overall therapeutic environment and encourages the partners to focus on productive changes in behavior and acceptance of personal responsibility.

The next step focuses on anger management techniques. Handouts and homework assignments which help them understand violent cycles and how to overcome them are given to the clients. The abuser is often not aware of his own anger nor the corresponding body and environmental cues to anger. Attending to non-verbal cues, being aware of his own feelings, and learning how to express these feelings in a more constructive way is emphasized. To create alternative ways of expressing anger, time is spent focusing on alternatives to violence. Other ways to ventilate anger that are not intimidating nor violent are modeled; for example, physical exercise, relaxation techniques, time-out periods, and desensitization.

Once a non-violent repertoire of behaviors to anger is established, we focus on communication. Fair fight rules are emphasized as a means of helping couples communicate better. Assumptions, "mind reading," and other maladaptive behaviors are pointed out with the use of psychoeducational techniques, role-playing, and modeling. Humor is often absent in abusive families. It is very important to be able to bring humor back into the relationship through the counseling lest the clients and the therapists become overwhelmed by the situation itself.

Finally, cognitive re-framing is utilized to reduce ritualistic behaviors, and to focus on irrational thoughts and beliefs. Rational-emotive therapy techniques (renewing the mind) are used to help the couple improve self-esteem by counteracting failure and worthlessness messages, and to confront rationalizations, denial, and tendencies to blame everyone else for the current situation and problems. Being able to assertively express feelings is especially important in abusive relationships, and these communication techniques are repeatedly emphasized. Problem solving techniques and conflict resolution methods are included in the therapy. By this point in the treatment, the couples are able to tolerate much more intense emotional expression without becoming abusive or defensive.

Self-esteem enhancement, which is a crucial factor in abusive situations, is also included. The couples are encouraged to discuss and think about their strengths, and to reinforce each other positively. Typically, these couples' definition of intimate behavior is strongly affected by their dysfunctional families of origin (Family Therapy Today. 1989).

Paul Bohovec, MSW, has developed a program in Fort Washington, PA called The Reduce Abuse Program (Project RAP). It has proven effective in treating abusive and/or overly controlling men through a group counseling approach. He states that "Safety precedes healing." That is, the treatment of the husband in group sessions is necessary prior to couple or family counseling.

In the first phase of the counseling, awareness of abusive behaviors (which include possessive, intrusive, demanding, controlling, and passive-aggressive behavior) are addressed, to include consequences for such behavior. They must learn how they give permission to themselves to act out.

In phase two, the working through of their feelings and developing accountability is accomplished. Group work emphasizes:

1. Recognizing difficult emotions and impulses and choosing not to act then out.
2. Acknowledging that their spouse has faults and may also be abusive.
3. Realize the danger of abuse, especially men to women.

4. Learn that there is no excuse for hitting or other physical violence.

Western societies, by and large socializes men to be dominant over women. Men who are emotionally insecure attempt to protect their vulnerability and shame by the mask of machismo and aggression. The man feels strong and in control when aggressive. Men are socialized that vulnerable, negative feelings need not be tolerated, and that aggressive explosions are just a part of our "maleness." Men must be taught to control and redirect aggressive impulses into constructive action.

For Class Discussion

1. Discuss the meaning of Reciprocal techniques. Why are they important?

2. What is meant by conjoint approach and when is it appropriate to use.

3. Of the Seven techniques listed, choose the three that you find most helpful, and discuss them.

"He executes justice for the orphan and the widow, and shows His love for the alien by giving him food and clothing."

Deuteronomy 10:18

*And above all, keep fervent in your love for one another,
because love covers a multitude of sins.*
I Peter 4:8
*Let him know that he who turns a sinner from the error of his way
will save his soul from death and will cover a multitude of sins.*
James 5:20

Chapter 14
Assisting to Rebuild Violent Family Systems

When a domestic crisis occurs within a marital relationship, there are several steps that one can take to assist in the resolution and rebuilding of their broken lives.

First things first. Remember our primary concern is safety for the clients, children first, and also ourselves. An assessment of the potential for physical violence within the family needs to be made at the onset. Whenever a spouse is in danger of continued physical abuse, it is strongly recommended that an intervention occur. In some cases, the police or other welfare agency may need to be contacted to give added reinforcement to the seriousness of the situation at hand. There are no scriptural prohibitions against self-protection excepting persecution for righteousness sake, which is hardly the case in marital/family violence. Where physical violence occurs, separation is generally necessary, and a healthy positive step in the recovery process.

There are several key things to be aware of during the crisis phase of the counseling process. They include:

1. Emotions

Emotions can run very high. Expect a lot of anger, tears, resentment, and bitterness between two people. This happens normally whenever two people cannot seem to get along together. In most domestic violence cases there will be heightened arousal of the victim and the abuser. Be careful not to get into the middle of a dispute, as it is a most dangerous position to be in.

2. Time

The time it takes to work through the crisis, let alone the longer process of restoration of the relationship must be considered. I have seen many cases last as long as 3 years before successful resolution has been gained. In any form of ministry we must be willing to weigh the cost before launching forward. Remember, these are very needy families with limited skills for problem solving, which is why referral to a specialized treatment center may be best, and group support is almost always required.

The role of a crisis counselor in the first stage of treatment is to open lines of communication that have been previously closed, with a hope to settle the situation down enough to make longer term interventions. To a great extent the counselors' role is to act as translator and mediator between the two combatants.

3. Blame

As previously mentioned, blame must be reduced or eliminated while responsibility for actions must be increased. Every effort must be made to reframe the focus of their passion towards problem resolution and clear communication.

Some things that are helpful include:

1. The counselor can provide a safe place for a controlled expression of emotions. The expression of feelings is not negative in and of itself. It can cause negative reactions however, some of which have been violent in the past. Again, caution is needed, as emotions in violent family systems run woefully high. Allow for the expression of feelings in a controlled manner, without the assassination

of character.
2. As a counselor, strategic neutrality is required. This means that the counselor must develop the skill of joining with empathy with all sides of the equation. Regardless of how injured one member of the family is versus another it is important to remember that there are no innocent victims (excepting with children).
3. Create a forum for them to be able to discuss things openly. Confidentiality and privacy is essential.
4. Encourage the couple to talk **with** each other, not **at** each other.
5. Remind them of the covenant that they have made with each other before God, especially if they are Christians.

There are certain things that one should not say in the midst of a marital or family crisis.

1. It is important to recognize that there are no "villains" or "victims." Do not take sides, or do so equally.
2. Do not assume responsibility for patching up someone's marriage. It is up to them and their level of commitment and hard work to change that will determine success or failure.
3. Do not underestimate the potential for acting out, even violence directed at the counselor in a domestic quarrel.
4. Be careful of unhealthy attractions, or dependencies, that could form between you and the counselee.
5. Romans 8:1 says that there is no condemnation to those who are in Christ Jesus. Those who have failed marriages or difficult family situations know their failures all too well and are often loaded down with guilt and shame. To add insult to injury is neither wise nor Christ like. They will need the tough love of a mature believer knowledgeable of the word to assist them through the morass of their wounded lives.

Helpful Techniques Towards Counseling Resolution

There are several techniques that can assist an individual to resolve problems rooted in the past. A primary goal would be to assist the clients in a search for truth, for the knowledge of truth acted upon can bring liberty (John 8:32). Once truth is revealed (of the sources of or roots of anger, insecurity, etc.) the need for forgiveness will become evident. Forgiveness is a commandment that the Lord gave. He said, "If you do not forgive, you will not be forgiven." It is therefore essential that forgiveness occur, and that trust, where possible and warranted can reemerge. Of course, forgiveness takes time, and often grieving is a necessary component of the process of letting go of the anger, hurt and pain.

My friend in the United States, Jan Frank has outlined a simple yet profound three phase approach to the healing of the wounds of incest. These stages are applicable to all types of counseling for domestic violence A *Door of Hope* by Jan Frank (Frank. 1990).

1. Face it

Facing the truth can be difficult for people in general, as we are all naturally defensive when caught in a situation where our self-esteem is threatened. When working with a domestic violence family where the loss of house and home is possible, the denial of responsibility and focus on self-survival is even more profound. However, we as counselors must not shy away from the ruthless pursuit of truth in the inner man of our clients. They must face the truth of their decisions and their consequences if help is to come. As long as the hurts and wounds are left in the dark and unattended they will fester until the rot destroys the client. It is only in the light that healing can occur.

2. Trace

Of the many questions that the counselor will ask himself or herself in the course of counseling (such as why did I choose this profession in the first place!), the chief inquiry will remain what things precipitated the family violence. In the case of child abuse, divorce, spousal abuse or the like, there are usually multiple causes of the problems presented. The origins may not be clear in the beginning, but we must trust the process, knowing that if we patiently search through assessment and questions well placed, we will learn the roots of the problems. Once found, the roots must be brought to the surface, the axe laid to the roots by the word of God, through healing prayer and repentance, while we must assist the clients to walk through the hurts until victory is experienced. We must take the time to pull back the curtain on the origins of the problems, including the possible multigenerational components. Through asking questions and allowing the individual to talk openly and freely we will eventually discover the truth.

3. Erase

To say good-bye to the hurts and problems that have been caused is a realistic goal. There are several methods that can be used to bring this to pass.

a. Letter writing or journaling

Assisting someone to write out what they feel and think, in the form of prayers to God or letters to those who have hurt them, can help them to process through the anger or hurt caused by abuse. A hopeful goal in the process is restoration and reconciliation. In some cases, a confrontation is required after perspective has been gained on the nuances of the abuse. However, caution is needed. In a majority of the cases, a confrontation would not be healthy, especially if the confrontation would hurt an innocent or if the person being confronted could again injure the client by denial or accusation. If the counselor is working with a perpetrator, the letter writing has a different focus, seeking to apologize and own responsibility for the victimization. For many, reparations and restitution of sorts must be made to the victims for true healing to occur for them. In either case, letter writing can be beneficial in processing their feelings in a positive way.

b. Role Playing

Assisting the individual to talk through their hurts is very helpful. One way to assist the client who has difficulty expressing emotions is through role-play. In role-play, the counselor takes a part in the play of the life of the client. For instance, the counselor might play the role of the client, and the client might play the part of the perpetrator. The purpose of the exercise might include the development of insight, or of empathy. Again, an assessment of the fragility of the client must be made to ensure that the technique will not cause further injury to the client. Seeking advice from an experienced supervisor might help to avoid painful mistakes.

These experiential things can help them move past the denial phase and help them in the grief process.

When counseling someone who has been abused, keep in mind the following things:

1. Trust is most difficult for a victim or a perpetrator to establish. Therefore, being supportive and empathetic is paramount. For trust to develop, the client needs consistency of care in the counseling process. The client is likely to challenge us in this regard, often eliciting similar feelings in us that are felt by those that have victimized them. These feelings are quite normal, and an indicator of the depth of counseling we are engaged in.
2. Denial is most strong in the victim who often has an apparent need to protect the victimizer. This comes from the intense threats that the victim has lived under over the

months or years of abuse. Telling the story is not easy, and distortion of the full story may be evident. Patience is needed until the whole truth can be told. One of the most difficult aspects of working with victims is the learned helplessness response. Their feelings of helplessness to assist themselves or change can be seen by the counselor as resistance. The resistance is caused because their will has been disabled due to the frequency and severity of the abuse. Given time, this can be overcome. It is worth waiting for and wading through.
3. Be prepared to assist, but do not become a rescuer. The temptation to become a Messiah for the victim is to be resisted as it is non-therapeutic for the client.
4. Look to the future while dealing with the past and present. Give a sense of hope, while encouraging longer-term therapy to correct with the damage caused by the abuse. Band-Aids are inadequate for the cure that is needed in the wounded soul of the victim.

Do not forget, more often than not, children suffer as victims of the psychological/ emotional abuse that is directed against a spouse. The needs of the child will always precede the needs of the adults.

For Class Discussion

1. Discuss the major modes of abuse counseling.

3. Discuss the place of marriage enrichment in the program of prevention.

4. How can marriages be rebuilt?

"Arise Shine; for your light has come, And the glory of the Lord has risen upon you. For behold, darkness will cover the earth And deep darkness the peoples; But the Lord will rise upon you, And His glory will appear upon you."

Isaiah 60:1-2

"Therefore do not be partakers with them; for you were formerly darkness, but now you are Light in the Lord; walk as children of Light."

Ephesians 5:7-8

"but if we walk in the Light as He Himself is in the Light, we have fellowship with one another, and the blood of Jesus His Son cleanses us from all sin."

I John 1:7

Is anyone among you suffering? Then he must pray. Is any cheerful? He is to sing praises.
Is anyone among you sick? Then he must call for the elders of the church;
and they are to pray over him, anointing him with oil in the name of the Lord:
and the prayer offered in faith will restore the one that is sick, and the Lord will raise him up; and if he has committed sins, they will be forgiven him.
Therefore, confess your sins to one another, and pray for one another so that you may be healed,
The effective prayer of a righteous man can accomplish much.
James 5:13 – 16

Chapter 15
The Secret Revealed:
Facing the Truth

David prayed, "Search my heart, O God and know my thoughts...see if there be any wicked way in me."(Ps.139:23) The very thought that the Family Secrets, often hidden for generations, might be revealed, creates trepidation in the heart of both victim and abuser. Because the family is all that they know, there is intense pressure to maintain the family unit. Children, especially, and the spouse who is battered, feel obligated to protect the family and victimizer, and abhor the possible responsibility of sending mom or dad "away". Yet to treat a family system, the truth must be faced. Though most difficult, with God's help and good clinical skills, the task of healing the broken and restoring the family can occur.

The Process

Even if a client is referred by a social service agency

for child or spousal abuse, the truth is not always clearly known. There is no psychological test that can predict a child or spousal abuser. The best predictor of present and future behavior is past behavior. One thing is for sure, without breaking through the denial, and facing the truth, the likelihood of repeated offenses is frighteningly high.

Breaking through

Frank was a 39-year old black man, father of six children, two by his first marriage and four by his second. The family had been referred for therapy to a Christian counselor because of their fervent religion and strong denial. Frank had been accused of repeated sexual assault on his oldest daughter, with clear but unprosecutable evidence of his guilt. Frank denied the abuse of the first session. I reviewed the reports and tried to directly confront Frank's denial. He was too "slick" for that, using the biblical term "under the blood" as his primary defense. As I listened to him relate, in a cocky and arrogant style, his innocence and disdain for the court and related agencies, I prayed for a word of wisdom to erode his denial. My theological arguments were well founded, but he remained smugly comfortable. I began to tell a story, with a moral of "where there's smoke, there's fire". I made this statement about ten times during the session. The family left, and I sensed that this case would be an up-hill battle. The next day I received a call from Frank. He was calling from the sheriff's office. He had voluntarily admitted his guilt, not only of abusing his daughter, but of having abused his son as well. He could not sleep as the Holy Spirit pounded the word of wisdom into him, convicting him of his of sin and "scaring me to death." With the denial removed, therapy could begin.

Depending on the situation, confrontation of denial and an honest search for truth can begin. Direct confrontation frequently creates defensiveness, and more indirect approaches are frequently needed. As a Christian Counselor, we are obliged to keep at the defensive system by analyzing it, challenging it, pointing out deception (in a loving way) in order to allow the Word of God to penetrate the soul.

Determination: Assessing the Problem

As mentioned previously, without a proper assessment, treatment is most difficult at best. Because of the nature of an abusive family system, multiple determinations of the problem may be necessary. In light of this, proper investigation into the family history, back two or more generations is helpful.

Generational Patterns

You will find in nearly 80% of family violence cases, one or both of the parents in the family had violent or abusive/neglectful parents. Therefore, most victimizers are, or were victims of a previous generation. This can be carried, as stated in Exodus 20, 34, "...unto the third and fourth generation.." Empathy for the victimizing of the past, and assisting the awareness of the patterns learned is a necessary and efficacious road of investigation. The dynamics that need to be observed and probed for include:

1. **Past abusive patterns** should be explored in detail. Often, due to poor communication and family denial, the patterns are not readily seen. A genogram or other such instrument can be helpful in gathering this information. Disclosing this information to the client can open doors for fruitful treatment.
2. **Triggers to abusive patterns**, often non-verbal cues, must be uncovered and brought to the surface. The stressors that release the rage or sexual acting out must be traced, and a full understanding of the causes of the abuse must be uncovered. Role-play of past (recent) incidents under strict

control can be helpful.
3. **Communication processes** have to be traced to determine how the family or couple remains stuck in their dysfunctional patterns. Especially look for, and describe in treatment, projections of blame, triangulation, unclear or mixed messages, and other faulty communications in the family.

Without proper determination of the real problems, one can wallow around in symptoms that are non-productive, prolonging the treatment process after determination of the problems. Discovery of the roots will take time, and must be traced systematically and thoroughly.

Ultimately, honesty is required for growth and change to occur. Honesty must be modeled, usually by the therapist, giving courage to the victim and victimizer alike.

Discovery: Uncovering the Roots

The Apostle Paul warned us not to allow "roots of bitterness" to enter into our hearts. In families victimized by violence and abuse, bitterness is quite likely.

Extreme anger and hurt, guilt and shame, are frequently at the root of family abuse. An individual has one of three choices to deal with these emotions:

1. Turn it to the outside and blame everyone for all the bad things that have happened to them.
2. Turn it inside, and blame themselves for everything bad that has happened.
3. Learn to express their anger (fear, guilt, etc.) using God given biblical principles, while discussing the best ways to handle anger and hurt.

The clients must acknowledge that the difficulties do go

deeper than immediate events. The patterns discovered through eroding the denial system must now be faced in all their impact. This will lead to the expression of anger and other emotions, which needs to be cautiously encouraged. Ultimately, the goal is the recognition of the "place of the devil," and removal of any bitterness through healing prayer. One way to process through the hurt so that bitterness can be removed is through existential exercises, such as writing letters to all perpetrators or co-perpetrators, (without mailing them, of course).

Dr. Dan Allender states that to ultimately overcome bitterness, we must learn to actually bless the other person. This is certainly not easy, but possible and required to grow in God. Further, he states "Real life requires death. Death involves the experience of suffering. Suffering is required for growth." All of us have something to overcome, and as the roots of bitterness are systematically removed, pain will be experienced. Yet pain is inevitable, and as a counselor we must compassionately work with our clients through the "valley of the shadow of death" (Allender. 1990).

Deliverance: Destroying Fortresses

In Luke 4, Jesus, speaking of himself and validating the prophecy of Isaiah, states, "The Spirit of the Lord is on me, because he has anointed me to preach good news to the poor. He has sent me to proclaim freedom for the prisoners and recovery of sight for the blind, to release the oppressed, to proclaim the year of the Lord's favor."

Jesus came to deliver those who are captive, to open prison doors, to comfort those who mourn. When He left the earth to ascend to His Father, He sent the Comforter, the Holy Spirit, for our direction, instruction and healing. As Christians, we have also been called to comfort, to fight for our brothers and sisters in distress. The power for deliverance (setting free) of those captives is available to us by the Holy Spirit.

When a multi-generational pattern of family abuse, especially sexual abuse, is evident, the breaking of these generational curses (an Old Testament concept, those of us in Christ are no longer under a curse, Gal 3:13) or patterns may be needed. This specialized area of ministry, a form of spiritual warfare, is a weapon that secular therapists can never know. We must use this wisely, so as to insure that no re-injury of the client occurs.

Prayer of Deliverance

Once general family patterns are uncovered, teaching on the plan and power of God to set us at liberty needs to be presented. This teaching should include:

Exodus 20:1-5
"Then God spoke all these words, saying, 'I am the Lord your God, who brought you out of the land of Egypt, out of the house of slavery. You shall have no other God's before me. You shall not make for yourself an idol, or any likeness of what is in the heaven above or on the earth beneath or in the water under the earth. You shall not worship them or serve them; for I the Lord your God, am a jealous God, visiting the iniquity of the fathers on the children, on the third and fourth generations of those who hate Me...'"

Exodus 34:6-7
"Then the Lord passed by in front of him and proclaimed, The Lord, the Lord God, compassionate and gracious, slow to anger, and abounding in lovingkindness and truth; who keeps lovingkindness for thousands, who forgives iniquity, transgression and sin; yet He will by no means leave the guilty unpunished, visiting the iniquity of fathers on the children and on the grandchildren to the third

and fourth generations."

Galatians 3:13

"Christ redeemed us from the curse of the Law, having become a curse for us – for it is written 'Cursed is everyone who hangs on a tree'"

Matthew 12:25-29, 43-45

"Any kingdom divided against itself is laid waste; and any city or house divided against itself will not stand. If Satan cast out Satan, he is divided against himself. how then can his kingdom stand? If I Beelzebub cast out demons, by whom do your sons cast them out? For this reason they will be your judges. But if I cast out demons by the Spirit of God, then the kingdom of God has come upon you."

"Now when the unclean spirit goes out of a man, it passes through waterless places seeking rest, and does not find it. Then it says 'I will return to my house from which I came;' and when it comes, it finds it unoccupied, swept, and put in order. Then it goes and takes along with it seven other spirits more wicked than itself, and they go in and live there. And the last state of that man becomes worse than the first. That is the way it will also be with this evil generation."

James 5:13-17

"Is anyone among you suffering? Then he must pray. Is anyone cheerful? He is to sing praises. Is anyone among you sick? Then he must call for the elders of the church and they are to pray over him, anointing him with oil in the name of the Lord; and the prayer offered in faith will restore the one who is sick, and the Lord will raise him up, and if he has committed sins, they will be forgiven him. Therefore, confess your sins to one another, and pray for one another so that you may be healed. The effective prayer of a righteous man can accomplish much."

Romans 12:12
"Rejoicing in hope, persevering in tribulation, devoted to prayer,"

II Corinthians 10:3-6
"For though we walk in the flesh, we do not war according to the flesh, for the weapons of our warfare are not of the flesh, but divinely powerful for the destruction of fortresses. We are destroying speculations and every lofty thing raised up against the knowledge of God, and we are taking every thought captive to the obedience of Christ, and we are ready to punish all disobedience, whenever your obedience is complete. (Spiritual warfare will continue. This is the mop-up campaign that will help us to develop godly self-respect)."

Through teaching, the counselor can provide a clear picture of the counselees responsibility in dealing with their past from a biblical viewpoint.

Once the time of study, meditation and instruction is complete, a two-hour session should be set for the prayer to break past bondages. You will need the guidance of the Holy Spirit, asking for clarity as you proceed. I encourage my clients to make a list of the hurts people may have caused, confessing any area of generational sin and systematically pray, agreeing with them for healing in the areas of brokenness. Often, as you pray, you will see God move in a very powerful fashion. This "file dump" will open the door to working through the roughest areas of their life. One caution must be stated. Except on rare occasions, this time of prayer can stir more than resolve. It is not a cure all, and much time will need to be spent working through the results of the past abuse, to learn how to establish new and positive relationships that are not abusive or neglectful. This dynamic process is available to us as Christian therapists, and is a powerful tool that we must be prepared to use as God leads us.

Dealing with the Thoughts

II Corinthians 10:3-6 speaks about a process most helpful for abuse victims and abusers alike, who struggle with residual negative thoughts that often plague them. The application of the scriptural principles is found here. The scripture provides four statements of therapeutic value.

1. **Our Warfare** - The warfare that is experienced in most clients is intense. It is difficult to imagine the level of hurt, sadness, shame and guilt that the client experiences. The fact of the flesh walk must be recognized. The pain, remorse, and fear are truly experienced, and are not to be minimized, yet the warfare is not in the flesh, but in the mind. Yet, the victory in Christ must also be clearly affirmed.
2. **The Power** - God has given us the power to overcome the hidden fortresses in our minds. Paul called our spiritual weapons, including prayer, meditation on God's Word, the gifts of the Holy Spirit, and confession, divinely powerful. Assisting your client to actively participate in the destruction of lies or negative beliefs that result from abusive situations is paramount in the healing process.
3. **Casting Down** - After the identification of the fortresses, they must be destroyed or cast down. This is done through confession and repentance. As we see the truth and "throw down" the lies, which are any thought or belief contrary to God's Word, they can experience the already provided for freedom in Christ'. We cannot cast things down or take the thoughts captive, the client must. The counselor becomes the primary motivator for the client to pursue this necessary

course.
4. **Punish** - To punish the disobedient thoughts means to stop indulging oneself in a narcissistic and non-productive pity party, but continuously remind the self that God has truly set us free. Our new creation image in Christ believed and experienced will truly punish the thoughts of the old nature and the devil alike.

Deliverance from bondage, whether soulish or spiritual, takes time, spiritual insight, certain gifting, and God's grace and mercy. Amazing results do occur in men and women who submit to God's prescribed process of liberation.

For Class Discussion

1. Discuss the concept of deliverance. Review the scriptures listed. Can you think of more scriptures that can be used in deliverance ministry?

2. What experience, if any, have you had with deliverance, casting down imaginations, etc.?

3. Discuss the idea of dealing with thought patterns from a biblical perspective.

"God forgave my sin, in Jesus name, I've been born again, in Jesus name, and in Jesus name, I come to you, to share his love, as he told me too. He said freely, freely, you have received, freely, freely give. Go in my name, and because you believe, others will know that I live."

Jesus Peoples days worship chorus.

"Wash me thoroughly from my iniquity, and cleanse me from my sin."

King David, Psalms 51:2

"Blessed are those who mourn, for they shall be comforted"

Matthew 5:4

*You blind Pharisee, first clean the inside of the cup and
of the dish, so that the outside of it may become clean also.
Woe to you, scribes and Pharisees, hypocrites! For
you are like whitewashed tombs, which on the outside appear
beautiful, but inside they are full of dead man's bones,
and all uncleanness.*
Matthew 23:26-27

*Therefore, having these promises, beloved, let us cleanse ourselves
from all defilement of flesh and spirit, perfecting holiness in the
fear of God.*
2 Corinthians 7:1

*If we confess our sins, He is faithful and righteous to forgive us
our sins, and to cleanse us from all unrighteousness.*
I John 1:9

Chapter 16
Decontamination:
The Cleansing

Along with honesty and prayer, there must come decontamination or a cleansing from the shame that accompanies abuse. The cleansing that comes through the talking, confession, and effective (to the mark) fervent prayer is step one. Step two, the deliverance through warfare prayer is vital. Third, you must assist the client to truly repent, or change their thinking, which will lead to a change in lifestyle.

Repentance

In spite of the abuse a person may have experienced, sin must be confessed, and our thoughts or beliefs must be changed. In II Corinthians 7:10, the Apostle Paul states that Godly sorrow, (sorrow for sin done or received, not for being caught), produces repentance <u>without</u> regret, leading to salvation (Sozo). The sorrow that is expressed must not be for sorrows sake, but must lead one to:

1. The truth, seeing the sin/situation as God does.
2. Without the continual regret or condemnation that people tend to feel due to prolonged abusive themes.

This process does not occur over night, in that Sozo or salvation, meaning to be whole or complete, is both a miraculous event of God's grace and mercy, and a progressive changing from glory to glory. Much of the time delay in the process is due to the reality of the negative seed that has been sown into the life of the abused, over time.

Sowing Death, Sowing Life

In the parable of the wheat and the tares (Matt. 13: 24-30, 36-43), Jesus speaks of two seeds being sown into the "field". The field has been interpreted as the world, or perhaps the church. However, with a certain amount of liberty the parable can be seen as analogous of the life of those who have been abused. The seed is one of two, either the good seed of the word of God, or the imitation seed of the devil, the later leading to bondage and death.

The devil's seed, or his word, are lies sown into the garden of our hearts. When abuse, neglect, negative words or statements are sown, often thousands of times, the resulting "weeds" or misbeliefs grow to choke the very life of the individual. Even Christians, those who know and understand the word of the Lord, may not be able to overcome in certain areas of life, not because of a lack of faith, but a lack of good seed versus bad. Therefore, gardening and pruning of the weeds and bushes (false beliefs and attitudes) is needed. Simply reading God's Word will not be sufficient to overcome the entrenched lies implanted over many months and years, especially when those very lies continue to be reinforced. Though the Word is quick and powerful, sharper than a two-edged sword (Heb.4:12), and can bring healing and restoration, we must have patience, as God works in the clients life according to His perfect timing. But rest assured, nothing is impossible with God. I have had the marvelous joy of watching the Lord heal and fully restore the most broken of people; God is faithful to his precious word.

Grief and Loss

The loss of innocence, and the childhood or marriage that could and should have been, is most difficult. Our clients must process through their sorrow, mourning their losses similar to that of a divorce or death. Much of the cleansing of a wounded heart will occur as the client mourns their loss, casting their burden on the Lord.

The Stages of Grief

Moving through the grief stages is not automatic. Your client will move through them in their own inimitable style, and in the timing of God. The circumstances of the loss will cause the client to move through the stages differently, depending upon their relationship with God, the kind and extent of the abuse, and their ability to embrace the pain they will be experiencing. Presented here is a brief review of the primary stages of grief.

Shock

The first stage of grief is shock. Shock is a numbness, which envelops the client, a most effective defense mechanism, necessary for surviving of the original event. Without it, the client may have never survived the trauma of the abuse. Shock is a physical experience in which the client loses a sense of the reality of the abuse, thus protecting himself or herself for a season. Many a client will also experience a form of amnesia regarding the events of abuse called a disassociative state. This psychological response to the immense stress of abuse is to be a temporary relief from the event, but often becomes permanent for the client.

Denial

Denial is the repression of the traumatic event or events over a longer period of time. Denial is the general inability of the client to face the truth of their victimization, or of being a victimizer. Denial for a short time is probably necessary and helpful, but becomes a mask that must be penetrated for therapeutic intervention to occur.

Fantasy Vs Reality

The third stage of transition of the grief process is the struggle between fantasy and reality. This can be viewed as a component of denial. The client will fantasize about how she or he wishes his/her family was, that the family will change, that the father will no longer come in at night, that the husband will not lose his temper any more. Reality is hard for most clients, but you must gently lead them to the facing of the whole truth if freedom is to be obtained.

Grief as a Release

In Jesus' reading of Isaiah 61 in the temple in Nazareth (Luke 4) He states that He had come to comfort all who mourn. However, for those who never mourn, there is rarely any comfort. Mourning is the releasing of the intense feelings that accompany the loss, in a way to bring relief to the client. The therapist is called upon to be the precipitator of the grief and the comforter as they mourn and process through the feelings of pain, usually through tears and much anguish. This is a most dramatic and sacred time for the client in the treatment process.

Learning to Live with the Memories

After the client has experienced, over a period of weeks, the flood of grief from the previous stage, the pain of grief begins to ease. However, this is often where the real battles for the soul begin. The work of restoration is far from over. The client must be reminded that the battle for the mind is yet to come, and to hang in there for the full process.

The memories can continue to plague and condemn the client for months after the treatment has begun. God made our minds with the ability to remember the most seemingly unimportant details of life. To truly forget everything that has happened to us is not realistic nor even desirable. The client has to learn to remember without condemnation, and without the pain associated. Like a scare, the reminder of the injury may always be with us, but the pain can be completely alleviated.

Acceptance and Affirmation

As the client processes through the grief cycle, they will eventually determine that "all things do work together for good to those who love the Lord". The beginning of therapy is not the time to share that Rhema! As their mind is renewed, they will be able to see how God has brought them through the valley of the shadow of death, and the fear and pain are now just faded memories. The cleansing of the heart of the person takes time, but the end result is a person or family fit for usage in the Kingdom of God.

For Class Discussion

1. Discuss the process of cleansing. What are the various steps?

2. Discuss the process in grief and loss. Discuss each part as described in the text.

3. Discuss the recovery process. Discuss each step.

4. Find several versus of scripture that seem to describe the process of restoration and recovery. Can you find Bible verses that deal with this part of the process?

Blessed are those who mourn, for they are comforted...but what happens to them who never mourn?

Matt. 5:4; DeKoven paraphrase

Therefore if anyone is in Christ, he is a new creature; the old things are passed away; behold, new things have come.
2 Corinthians 5:17

Chapter 17
Direction:
New Beginnings

The overall goal of counseling is the restoration of the abuser and the victim. There are several steps in concluding this book that should be considered in finalizing the recovery or restoration process.

1. The Word of God is a dynamic force that must be a part of your counseling process. This is especially true as you attempt to wrap-up the formal counseling contract. The client must be taught the principles of the word, and how to find answers for him/her self. What is learned in the counseling milieu is nearly as important as therapy itself.
2. Assist the client to "fish" for themselves in the word and through such activities as journaling. The dependency that naturally occurs between the client and the therapist must be slowly weaned. The ultimate statement of health is that the client is now dependent on the Lord Jesus Christ and His Body (in local expression) rather than the therapist.
3. Forgiveness is an absolute necessity, and yet cannot be forced. Remember that it is a process, one commanded by the Lord, but use wisdom in pushing for it.
4. Leave an open door for a return to your office if necessary. It is quite normal to have occasional visits for a check up, as long as it does not become a regular checkup.
5. Acknowledge the dignity of the client, as they have completed a phase of their ultimate healing. Be careful to

remind them that perfection is designed for a very few; primarily Messiahs!
6. Insure that the love of Jesus will never fail. They are co-inheritors with Christ, and are commendable to Him.

The journey with the abused or the abuser is often long and difficult. The pitfalls at times make the journey seem terribly long. But trust in the Lord, for if you have been placed in a position of ministry, having been properly trained to minister to the wounded, you can have confidence that the Lord will assist you beyond your seeming limit. I am never more amazed than when that which is impossible with man becomes possible, even easy with God.

Family violence is a scourge in the land, and the church is well positioned to minister with great effect to the wounded and the wounder alike. The ministry of compassion and mercy, mixed with wisdom stemming from knowledge and understanding can be most powerfully used in our day. Jesus stated that he who is forgiven much, loves much. Nothing could be truer than when an abuser or victim becomes healed by the power of God well applied through the ministry of counseling.

For Class Discussion

1. Find some scriptures to help a client come to a place of forgiveness.

"True fellowship exists when people are at least as interested in the affairs of others as they are in their own affairs. By contrast, a major hindrance to fellowship is self-pity and/or the desire for sympathy. People who are mostly concerned about their own hurts and needs cannot commit themselves to true fellowship. Koinonia demands a genuine interest in the affairs of others.

Dr. Barry Chant, The Church, Vision Publishing, 1992

"Now on the last day, the great day of the feast, Jesus stood and cried out, saying, If anyone is thirsty, let him come to Me and drink. He who believes in Me, as the scripture said, From his innermost being will flow rivers of living water."

John 7:37-38

The Church is a religious home, a sanctuary for worship, a school for religious instruction, a fighting unit for the new world that is building. It is a social center of the highest type, since it gathers into relations of mutual helpfulness people of every age and condition, and since it adds to the attractions of the ordinary club of power or religion and the generous sympathies of the altruistic impulse. The Church is the most broadening and catholic organizations among men, since its vision is to the ends of the world whither the gospel is being carried, and since its citizenship is in heaven as well as in the earth.
Worth M. Tippy

Chapter 18
The Church's Response:
A Wake Up Call

Let me illustrate.[5] It was about three a.m. when the phone rang. As I rubbed the sleep from my eyes, I listened intently to a story that I have heard only too often. Late the evening before, a rather well known member of a local church had been arrested. He was being held in custody for alleged sexual abuse against some children in the same church. The pastor knew all the principle parties well, and felt caught. He could clearly sense the outrage of the parents of the children who were abused. He was concerned for the children's welfare. He also experienced a sense of outrage at his friend, a man he had ministered to and fellowshipped with, who had allegedly committed this horrible sin.

He also remembered the Christian commitment of Mr. Jones. He must be terribly frightened, and what about Mrs. Jones? What response would she have? Finally, he had many questions regarding his own response. What would his church think? What

---

[5] All illustrations are true, though many specifics have been rearranged to ensure anonymity.

would the Lord do? Excellent questions. Difficult answers!

After I got over my own feelings of shock and anger, (why me, Lord? I really needed some sleep!) I began to explore with this very caring and sensitive pastor some of the options that he and the church might exercise. I have since found that the options we explored together to be typical of most evangelical churches, and have listed them in their most often used order.

1. **The Ostrich Approach is to**: Bury it and hide. Pretend as though it didn't happen. Think of the harm that could come if anyone found out. A former colleague once told me of a certain pastor's fears about exposing problems in the church. He likened it to the picking up of a rock. When you do so, the bugs start crawling out! "Better to keep the rock where it is" the pastor stated (and the inherent church problems) "than to expose people's problems" (for fear of the repercussions). "Let's not let anyone know. We don't want anyone to be hurt." Unfortunately, this was the approach that the local church board (who overruled the pastor) used to deal with the problem. The results were devastating for Mr. Jones, the family involved, and for the church as a whole.

2. **The Cancer Approach is**: Mr. Jones has obviously sinned grievously, guilty until proven innocent! The thought was, "If we continue to offer fellowship to him, the results could be devastating. We must cut him off and give total support to the victims only." This would certainly be a better solution than option #1. This option does eliminate the "problem" in a hurry. In a hurry is right! Usually it is a hasty decision made out of fear. The use of this option offers much needed support for the victim. It is direct and decisive. But what about Mr. Jones? Where is the compassion he needs? Yes, perhaps he has sinned. But in spite of the ugliness of this type of sin, God continues to love Mr. Jones, and desires to restore him. There are no

doubt necessary legal consequences for his action. Yet, he still needs restoration through the body of Christ.

3. **The Healing Community**: Mr. Jones indeed had sinned in a most destructive and despicable fashion. The sexual abuse of children in our society is one of the leading causes of emotional problems in adults today. The church is not exempt from this sin, as we are now becoming only too aware. Yet, even in the case of sexual crime and sin, there are some basic principles of operation that we must exchange in order to fulfill our responsibility in Christ.

   a. First, we must confront the situation head on. We must know the facts as best we can. Yet, we must do so with an open mind.
   b. Second, if possible, we must talk with the responsible parties, offering comfort and support, motivated by love. Although Jesus never excused sin or the sinner, He was willing to love and pardon. Each individual needs to be heard and offered clear opportunity for restoration through repentance.
   c. Third, we must keep all communication confidential, and where necessary, squelch rumors and gossip. There is a natural human tendency to want to know all the details.
   d. Fourth, we must offer continued ministry from the church so that continued restoration might occur. This could include ministry in areas of victim assistance (church support for needed counseling, etc.) and prison outreach. Whatever we do, when one of our own is wounded, even if self-inflicted, we must be willing and able to bind up their wounds and allow healing to occur. We must not shoot our wounded!

Most of our churches today are ill prepared to handle such emergencies which will inevitably happen within the family, and the family of God. Few churches have trained laity or pastoral staff who can help in times of real crisis. Yet, it is in the time of crisis that we are most open to the love and grace of the Lord Jesus Christ. We as His people have been left with the responsibility of ministering to the family when they are between the "rock and the hard place." I have often felt that, it is precisely there, between the rock and the hard place that the love of Christ, carefully and judiciously applied, can most fully and completely "heal the broken hearted and set the captive free." The Lord has charged us with His ministry of reconciliation (II Cor. 5:18-19). Are we willing to take a stand for Him?

For centuries marital and child abuse have been "unmentionable" sins. The church, like society as a whole, has ignored the problem and maintained a conspiracy of silence. Victims of this kind of violence feel humiliated. Many feel betrayed by God, experiencing a loss of faith and trust. In the church few have responded effectively, many have inadvertently denied the gravity of the problem, or even made it worse.

The church needs to take a definite theological and spiritual stand on the issue of marital violence and child abuse.

Symptoms of Abuse

Symptoms of abuse to which pastors and church members need to be aware include:

Patterns of absenteeism or interruption of regular attendance at Sunday services, choir practice, group meeting and other regular church activities can all be symptoms of an abusive situation.

Any change in patterns such as not sitting in one's regular place in church, avoiding friends, leaving before the end of the service or immediately after, etc. can also suggest problems.

A sudden change in appearance, such as radical changes in clothing (i.e. from well kept to sloppy, conservative to seductive) or a change in makeup from no makeup to extreme makeup is a possible sign that something is wrong.

Such things as refusing to see the pastor or speaking for the wife on the phone could be an indication that abuse is happening.

There are many other evidences that should receive attention such as: Showing up at church at unusual times. Physical changes including new glasses, dental work (maybe due to broken teeth), hairstyle (covering bruises), obvious bruises and injuries such as burns or broken bones.

Suggestions for Pastors and Counselors Responding to Victim's of Spousal Abuse

When a Pastor is told that abuse is occurring with one of his/her parishioners, it should always be taken seriously. If the wife says she is being abused, believe her. It is difficult to accept that things like abuse happen in church families, but they do. If battered women are not taken seriously, the sin will continue.

If it is perceived that the woman is in immediate danger, she should be offered a place to stay for a night or two, until a suitable place can be found for her.

The one thing that a battered wife needs most in a time of crisis is a listening ear and understanding. Understanding is much better than advice. Just sharing the frustration and fear that a victim is experiencing can help resolve some of the confusion. Ministers and counselors (lay or professional) must not only be approachable, but they must be shock proof. Reactions of shock or embarrassment will reinforce the feelings of shame being experienced by the victim. The victim is in need of support and the courage to take appropriate action.

In counseling a victim, it is important to help them see that they is not to blame for their husband's violent behavior (to some extent she may carry fault, but now is not the time to present that possibility). She needs to realize that her husband's behavior is wrong regardless of what may have precipitated the outburst. The Victim should not be made to feel that she must return home

Immediately without some guidance regarding a reasonable approach to a way of confronting him with his need to change.

The counselor is to present the possibility of choices: that battered women have options. She must be helped to make her own choices. Although the counselor may feel that she knows what she should do, it is important that she realize that their primary responsibility is to support and guide. It is the victims responsibility to take action.

A part of the counseling responsibility is to help restore or repair lowered self-esteem. A battered woman needs to see herself as Christ sees her. Pointing out scripture verses that demonstrate God's love for her can do this. These include:

Rom. 5:8 "But God commendeth His love toward us in that, while we were yet sinners, Christ died for us."

Rom. 8:37 "In all these things, we are more than conquerors through Him that loved us."

I John 3:1 "Beloved, what manner of love the Father has bestowed upon us, that we should be called the sons of God."

I John 4:10 "Herein is love, not that we loved God, but that He loved us, and sent His Son to be the atoning sacrifice for our sins."

It is always advisable to direct the victimized woman to a support group, either in the local church or in another church or agency.

Responding to Abusing Men

The first and foremost priority is that **the violence must stop.** The man must be made to understand that the violent behavior can not go on. His rationalizations must not be accepted. Even if he feels extreme stress because of his work, abuse of alcohol, his wife's nagging, etc., the violence is not acceptable.

The man must be held accountable for his actions. His promises to change are usually a part of the cycle of violence, unless they are accompanied by concrete actions, such as seeking counseling, etc. He needs to be convinced that he can change.

The counselor must not take his word that the violence has stopped. Abusers must be constantly watched. Check with the abused partner and establish some system of accountability with other men in the church.

The Role of the Church

As Christians, we have a responsibility to do everything we can to assist repentant abusive men along the road to recovery. What better testimony is there to the power of God than the healing of someone deemed as hopeless.

Wife battering hurts. As long as it is kept silent it will go on hurting. The church has a ministry to perform, but how can we respond to the cry of the victims we don't (or won't) see?

For the abused wife, the church should be a place of refuge and aid while she searches through her maze of confusion.

We can help the batterer by confronting him with the reality of what he is doing and by helping him understand the meaning of marriage as it was ordained by God.

To the entire family, we can offer encouragement, support, and a working model of a healthy family relationship. Christ's loving compassion compels us to do no less.

Yes, there is hope for the battered wives, and battering husbands too. Only through the healing hands of the Lord Jesus Christ does complete recovery happen, and it is our hands that the Lord uses to reach out and help the hurting.

Hebrew 4:15 "For we have not an high priest which cannot be touched with the feelings of our infirmities."

Isaiah 50:4 "God has given me the tongue of the learned that I should know how to speak a word in season to him that is weary."

John 21:15-16 "...lovest thou me more than these? ...Feed my lambs."

For Class Discussion

1. Discuss the church's role in dealing with family violence.

2. What symptoms of abuse should the church be concerned about?

3. Discuss the scripture in the text as it refers to the church's role. Can you list others?

4. How can the church help abusing men?

5. What can the church do to help battered wives or women in general?

Case Studies

Case Study 1

The Harmons, Bill and Jan, ages 43 and 41, two children, John and Jill, ages 16 an 17.

Statement of the Problem

The Harmons were referred for counseling by their Pastor. The family was seeking counseling due to the eldest son's physical threats against the mother, physical assault and inappropriate sexual suggestiveness towards the sister.

Initial Interview

The family was closed, unemotional (except for the father's occasional expressions of rage against the son). The mother related that all was wonderful in the family until John began acting out 6 months prior. She described the family as Christian, and quite normal. The daughter was slightly withdrawn, and somewhat depressed. She stated that she was only in counseling to support or help her mother. John remained quiet and nearly detached from the family, showing a little smile on his face.

History

It took some time to gain a sense of trust in the family. In separate interviews with the family, John and Jill presented quite differently. Both felt that mom and dad had the real problem, and John had threatened mom but only after mom screamed at him. Mom admitted to "losing it" once in a while, but fears her son's power. After the initial statement about John's sexual inappropriateness it was never discussed again.

I focused the counseling on the generational pattern of Mom and Dad in their families of origin. Both had initially related happy homes. After some probing, the underlying truth was uncovered. Jan had been sexually abused and traumatized by her father from age 4 until age 20, six months prior to her wedding. She had never revealed this secret to anyone, and was most fearful and enraged. In a counseling session, after giving her some time to process the pain of the abuse, she chose to tell her husband. He showed little sympathy for Jan, merely intense anger towards the perpetrator. As I explored this further, Bill revealed that he had also been sexually abused and raped by friends of his older brother when he was 12 years of age. Neither knew of the others abuse until revealed in the counseling process. Both were unconsciously projecting their fears on their son, who happened to look like Jan's father.

Treatment Process

Once our focus changed from the son (who was acting out some of the family pathology, mom's fear of her daughter being abused) we began to see how the pain of the generational abuse had set into motion beliefs and needs that were highly dysfunctional. Once the secrets were revealed, grief work was begun and worked through, and communication systems re-worked, the family began to move towards a healthy adjustment.

For Class Discussion

1. Discuss the case study, especially with regard to the how you might treat the situation.

Case Study 2

Melissa, age 26, a single Caucasian female, and a recent Christian, came for counseling for low self-esteem, symptoms of co-dependency, and extreme anxiety. Her former live-in boyfriend that she continued to date was the focus of her counseling complaint. He was a recovering crystal methamphetamine addict, who had been in jail on a drug related charge and released only three months prior. He was most repentant, and had begged her to continue to see him. She was confused and needed advice.

Melissa related that she needed help in deciding whether to marry her boyfriend or not. She had dropped him before he was sent to jail, but still felt she should give it another chance. She had dropped another boyfriend before this one, three months before. She was to be married but was too attached to the present one. She presented as an intelligent, yet extremely confused young lady.

History

Melissa was the middle child (older brother, younger sister) of an alcoholic family system (father). Though she had been treated well as a child, she frequently observed her father physically and verbally assault and abuse her mother. She had left the home to go to college, which she graduated from. She was presently in an outstanding job.

Present

She had broken up with her present boyfriend due to his drug usage, episodic violence, excessive pornography addiction, and extreme manipulative and controlling behavior. Further, when he stated she no longer wanted to see him (in the past) he would threaten her or threaten to commit suicide. She feared that he might do just that, and it would be all her fault. Finally, she believed that

Patterns of Destruction

as a Christian she was obligated to work things out if possible because she had slept with him. She was clearly conflicted between co-dependency and desire for her independence life.

Course of Treatment

At Melissa's request, we included her boyfriend in a session every other week.

Our focus was "pre-marital" counseling, with a goal of preparing them for marriage. The more we discussed the attributes of maturity and the biblical grounds for marriage, the potential spouse became increasingly agitated. He had two "slips" of pornography and drugs, but she continued to "forgive" him.

After six months, she decided that he was too much like her father (she had not seen the similarity before). His response was similar to the past, but this time she did not give in to his threats, even calling the police when he tried to break down the door of her flat.

Melissa is still single, actively involved in her church. She is dating cautiously, and is in a support group for co-dependents and adult children of alcoholics. Her prognosis is good. Her ex-boyfriend still tries to "rehook" her, unsuccessfully.

For Class Discussion

1. Discuss the various aspects of Case Study 2.

2. Was the course of treatment adequate or can you think of other things that could have been done to assist her?

BIBLIOGRAPHY

Allender, Don B. (1990). *The Wounded Heart: Hope for Victims of Childhood Sexual Abuse.* Colorado Springs: Navpress.

Allender, Don B. (1992). *The Wounded Heart: Work Book.* Colorado Springs: Navpress.

Brewer, C. A. (1990). *Family Violence.* British Columbia: Vine Publications:B.C.

Carter, William Lee. (1991). *Learning More About Family Commun-ication.* Texas: Ralph Publishing Co.

John D. Van de Kempe, Attorney General. (1988). Child Abuse Prevention Handbook, Crime Prevention Center. Office of Attorney General,

DeKoven, S. (1994). *I Want to be like You, Dad.* Ramona, CA: Vision Publishing, Inc.

Family Therapy Today. 1989.

Finklehor, D. (1984). *Child Sexual Abuse.* New Therapy Research, NY: Free Press.

Frank, J. (1995) *A Door of Hope.* Nashville, TN: Thomas Nelson Inc.

Gelles, R. (1992) *Breaking Destructive Patterns: Multiple Strategies for Treating Partner abuse.* NY: Free Press.

Gelles, R. (1979) *Family Violence.* Beverly Hills: Sage Publications.

Gill, D. (1978) *Violence Against Children: Physical Child Abuse in the United States.* M.A.: Harvard University Press

Goldberg, H. *Rage -- Its Many Faces.*

"A Group Therapy Program That Treats Batterers." *In The Interchange for Mental Health Professionals.* January, 1994.

Hansen, James C. (1982) *Clinical Approaches to Family Violence.* MD: Aspen Publication.

Hensen, J. ed. *Clinical Approaches to Family Violence.*

Holmes and Rabe. *The Social Readjustment Scale.*

Humphries, J. (1993) From a Seminar "Conference on Trauma and Sexuality. San Diego.

Kempe, et al. *Helping the Battered Child and His Family.*

Lee, William F. (1989) *Stress: The Inevitable - Peace: The Possibility.* WC: F.L.E.A.,Inc.

Mallory, James and Kubetine, Cynthia. (1992) *Learning More About Sexual Abuse.* TX: Rapha Publishing.

Martin, Grant L. (1990) *Counseling for Family Violence and Abuse.* TX: Word, Inc.

McGee, R. and Schaumburg, H. (1990) *Renew: Hope for Victims of Sexual Abuse.* TX: Rapha Publishing.

Oscar, L. (1965) *La Vida: A Puerto Rican Family in the Culture of Poverty.* NY: Vantage Books.

Selye, H. (1978) *The Stress of Life.* IA:McGraw-Hill

Treatment of Families in Conflict. (1983) The Committee on the Family Group for the Advancement of Psychiatry, Netherlands: Jason Aronson, Inc.

Additional References

American Psychiatric Association, (1986). *Diagnostic and Statistical Manual.* 3rd ed. revised, Washington, D.C.

Beck, A. 1974. *Love is Never Enough.* NY:Harper Paperbacks.

Blumstein, P. and Schwartz, P. (1983). *American Couples.* New York: Morrow.

Bockus, F. (1980). *Couple Therapy.* New York: Aronson.

Bowman, Murry, M.D. (1978) *Family Therapy in Clinical Practice.* New York: Aronson.

Brammer, Lawrence M, and Shostrom, Everett, L. (1982). *Therapeutic Psychology: Fundamentals of Counseling and Psychotherapy, 4th ed.* New Jersey: Prentice Hall, Inc.

Browne, Angela, (1987). *When Battered Women Kill.* New York: The Free Press.

Budman, S. (ed). (1981). *Forms of Brief Therapy.* New York: Guilford Press.

Cameron, N. (2nd Ed.) (1985). *Personality Development and Psychopathology.* Boston: Houghton Mifflin.

Davidson, Terry. (1978) *Conjugal Crimes: Understanding and Changing the Wifebeating Pattern.* New York: Hawthorn Books. 1978.

Corsini, R. (1973). *Current Psychotherapies.* Itasca:F.E. Peacock, Publishers.

Filsinger, E. E. and Lewis, R. A. (Ed.), (1981). *Assessing*

Marriage: New Behavioral Approaches. Beverly Hills: Saga.

Goldstein, A. J. and Rosenbaum, A. (1982). *Agress-less: How to Turn Anger and Aggression Into Positive Action.* Englewood Cliffs: Prentice Hall.

Gottman, J., Notarius, C.I., and Markman, H. (1976). *A Couple's Guide to communication.* Champaign: Research Press.

Guerin, Philip J. Jr., M.D. (Ed). (1976). *Family Therapy: Theory and Practice.* New York: Basic Books, Inc.

Guerin, Philip, J. Jr. et. al. (1987).*The Evaluation and Treatment of Marital Conflict: Four Stage Approach.* New York: Basic Books, Inc.

Gurman, A. S. (Ed.) (1985). *Casebook of Marital Therapy.* New York: Guilford.

Langley, R. & Levy, R. (1977) *Wife Beating: The Silent Crisis.* New York: E. P. Dutton.

Martin, D. *Battered Wives.* (1976) San Francisco: Glide Publications.

Moore, D. ed. *Battered Women.*(1979) Beverly Hills: Sage Publications.

Minuchin, Salvador. (1974). *Families and Family Therapy.* MA: Harvard University Press.

NiCarthy, G. (1982). *Getting Free -- A Handbook for Women in Abusive Relationships.* Seattle: The Seal Press.

Nichols, William C. and Everett, Craig A.(1986) *Systemic Family*

Therapy: An Integrative Approach. New York: Guilford Press.

Pizzey, E. (1977). *Scream Quietly or the Neighbors Will Hear.* New Jersey: Ridley Enslow, Publishers.

Robards, A. R. (Ed.) (1984). *Battered Women and Their Families: Intervention Strategies and Treatment Programs.* New York: Springer.

Roy, M. ed. (1977) *Battered Women: A Psychological Study of Domestic Violence.* New York: Van Nostrand-Reinhold co.

Russell, D.E.H. (1982).*Rape in Marriage.* New York: Macmillian.

Satir, V. (1967). *Conjoint Family Therapy.* Palo Alto: Science and Behavior Books.

Sherman, Robert and Fredman, Norman. (1986). *Handbook of Structured Techniques in Marriage and Family therapy.* New York: Brunner/Maxel.

Sonkin, D. and Durphy, M. (1983). *Learning to Live Without Violence: A Book for Men.* San Francisco: Volcano Press.

Stacey, W. (1983) *The Family Secret: Domestic Violence in America.* Boston: Beacon Press.

Straus, M.A., Gelles, R.J., and Steinmetz, S.K. (1980). *Behind Closed Doors: Violence in American Families.* New York: Doubleday.

Stuart, R. B. (1980). *Helping Couples Change.* New York: The Guilford Press.

Wile, D.E. (1981). *Couples Therapy: A Non-Traditional Approach.* New York: Wiley

Appendices

Scriptures on Husband & Wife Relationships i
Vision Publishing Book List ii

Appendix i

Your word I have treasured in my heart, That I may not sin against You.
Psalms 119:11

Scriptures on Husband and Wife Relations

Provided here is a listing of key scriptures for husbands and wives. The reader is encouraged to look them up for your better understanding and equipping.

Gen 1:26-28

Gen 2:7

Gen 2:18

Gen 2:21-23

Gen 2:25

Gen 3:1-21

Exo 20:5, 12, 17

Psa 37:1

Prov 5:15-17, Prov 6:32, Prov 31:10-31

Mat 5:27-28, Mat 5:31-32, Mat 12:25-29, Mat 12:43-45

Mark 3:23-27, Mark 7:14-23

John 5:19-24

Rom 7:1-4, Rom 8:1, Rom 12:1-2, Rom 13:1-10

1 Cor 7:1-17, 1 Cor 13:1-13

Gal. 3: 13, Gal 3:28-29, Gal 5:14-21, Gal 6:1-10

Eph 4:11-32, Eph 5:15-16, Eph 5:21-22, Eph 5:4

Phil 2:3-11

Col 3:5-15, Col 3:18-21 .

Heb 12:1-3, Heb 4:12-13

James 1:19, James 1:20-25, James 4:1-10, James 5:13-16

1 Pet 1:13-16, 1 Pet 2:9-10, 1 Pet 3:1-9, 1 Pet 5:6-8

1 John 1:1-4, 1 John 1:6-10, 1 John 2:7-11, 1 John 3:10-11, 1 John 4:7-8

Appendix ii

Vision Books by Dr. Stan E. DeKoven

1. Addiction Counseling
2. Assessment in Counseling
3. Catch the Vision
4. Christian Education
5. Crisis Counseling
6. 40 Days to the Promise
7. Fresh Manna
8. From a Father's Heart
9. Grief Relief
10. Homiletics
11. I Want To Be Like You Dad
12. Journey Through the New Testament
13. Journey Through the Old Testament
14. Journey to Wholeness
15. Keys to Successful Living
16. Laws of Christ
17. Leadership in the Church
18. Living Fruitfully
19. Marriage and Family Life
20. New Beginnings
21. On Belay! Introduction to Christian Counseling
22. Parenting on Purpose
23. Patterns of Destruction
24. Prelude to a Requiem
25. Research Writing made Easy
26. Setting the House in Order
27. Starting Out Right
28. Strategic Church Administration
29. Supernatural Architecture
30. That's the Kingdom
31. The Bible in Counseling
32. The Healing Community
33. The Overcomer's Life
34. Transferring the Vision
35. Twelve Steps to Wholeness
36. Visionary Leadership
37. What Does God Want